Understanding the
# DESTRUCTIVE POWER
## —OF—
# ASSUMPTION
### And How to Control it

## GREGORY DOLLAR

*Understanding The Destructive Power of Assumption
and How To Control It*
by Gregory Dollar

Printed in the United States of America

ISBN  9781615793235

www.xulonpress.com

**THIS BOOK IS DEDICATED** to my God, my most precious children and my love, Stacy. You have stuck with me through it all. There is no greater support I have experienced than through you. Thank you so much for believing in me. Your confidence in my desire to fulfill God's call on my life is priceless. I love you very much.

Also, to my parents who raised me from seventeen and taught me God's Word, you will always be my inspiration as I continue to accomplish God's plan for my life. To my good friends that have sacrificed their time to make this possible, thank you.

# CONTENTS

# ACKNOWLEDGEMENTS

**I WOULD LIKE TO** acknowledge those that worked countless hours on this project.

To the graphic designers, my son, Blaine Dollar and my great friend, Nigel Hemby, your creativity is inspiring, and your dedication appreciated. May God bless you richly.

To the proofreaders and editors, Stacy McPherson, Monica Russell and Anna Bailey Gibson also photography by Karen Styes. Your commitment, professionalism and time spent to make this project a success are invaluable; it could not have been done without you. I thank God for you and pray His blessings to abundantly flow in your lives.

To the publication team, thank you Xulon Press for making it possible to spread the gospel, powerful messages and stories through self-publishing.

I am thankful to you all for your support, enthusiasm and commitment.

# INTRODUCTION

**I HAVE BEEN IMMERSED** in work on my new book Love In The Darkness, which is an aggressive account of my life and all the struggles I have overcome, from a family of physical abuse and drugs to adoption into a new family in ministry. Unfortunately, the challenges and trials in my young life did not end there. Continually searching for my station in life and what plans God had for my future, I ended up in places that I did not belong and did things that were a far cry from my new upbringing and moral standards. It is a unique story which will evoke both tears of sadness and tears of joy. It will help you to see you are not alone in this world, and whatever comes your way, you can overcome it, especially with God's help. As it often does for most of us, my daily life revealed to me an idea, a truth.

While working on the book, I encountered one of the worst breakups I had ever experienced. Many weeks went by before we spoke to each other, and it was dreadfully heartbreaking. Most of my life, I had a fairly strong and sometimes cold heart where relationships were concerned. This one took me by surprise. Once we began communicating again, talking about what happened and discussing whether or not our relationship would ever be salvageable, we came to the conclusion we both assumed too much about each other. We still had much to discuss. In short time, we reestablished our relationship, and now it is exponentially more rewarding.

While assumption was fresh in my mind, I started to review what had previously been written in Love In The Darkness and began preparing for the next chapter. Looking at the outline and considering all the things that had happened in the past, I saw a major pattern in all the problems I had faced throughout my life. Almost every issue involved someone making assumptions; most of the time, it was me. I dug deeper and deeper into the subject, and it simply  ignited in my heart as I started to see how destructive assumption could become. I immediately saw a change in my life for the better as I became more aware of it lurking around every corner and made a decided effort to address it head-on.

It is my sincere desire to share my experiences and

knowledge in this area, open people's eyes to see such a stealthy enemy in our everyday lives and to be able to tackle it to the ground, never to devastate us again.

There are countless and exceptional books, CDs, videos out there, and great men and women who teach on many subjects which will help you live life to its fullest. We constantly look for solutions to fix our problems, be better with our finances and enjoy a healthier lifestyle. Often, we even search for pathways to a better relationship with God. This is not an instruction on managing better finances, family, healing or any common themes you may have heard, but if you take a hold of this message about assumption, every area of your life will dramatically change for the better. I continually aspire to tackle the most uncommon areas we most neglect, so you may amplify your efforts in the aspects of your life you desire to develop the most.

My purpose for this book is purely to help you observe assumption in a clearer way. It has many incarnations, which we'll cover, and you may interpret ideas differently than I or someone else. It is not imperative you necessarily concur with everything I state, but it is more crucial to me you become more conscious of the importance of acknowledging assumption. My objective is for you to understand some of the elements that make it so dangerous; I want to aid you to become more keenly aware of it when assumption insinuates itself in your life and offer ways to handle it. I will also suggest some fundamental things you can do to overcome this hazardous hindrance known as assumption.

Though this book is geared towards the Christian community, my friends and family, I trust this information will inspire anyone. In 1 Timothy 1:15, the apostle Paul states he is the chief of sinners. I believe I have equally become the chief of mistakes over the course of my forty years. I have learned many lessons and pray you will learn from them as well. I believe this is a great book for teenagers; it will help prepare them for the future ahead. If my insight allows one person to live and enjoy a better life, this book is well worth all I have gone through to get it into your hands. One word from God can change your life forever. I believe the one word I'm inspired to share with you will make it happen.

## CHAPTER 1

# WHAT IS ASSUMPTION?

**ASSUMPTION** has become an exceptionally powerful word to me and has pierced the very depths of my heart within the past year. In all the days of my life prior, never once did I recognize how vicious it had been. I have come to realize in an incredibly short time how often it is ignored by most people.

Assumption is a critical tool of the human intellect, giving us the ability to process our thoughts. It serves as a link between our rational and emotional thinking processes, a necessary instrument for our survival and a part of what makes us who we are. When we go to bed each night, we assume we'll wake up the next morning. When we flip a switch, we assume the light will turn on. When we take medicine for our headache, we assume the pain will go away. Yet, when it involves our social life, assumption is a whole different matter altogether. It is this element of assumption, if not controlled, that can be potentially dangerous, even deadly.

The noun assumption is related to the verb assume, which has various fascinating meanings. Assume can mean to take the place, command or obligation of another, such as assuming the Executive Producer position, because the other individual has gone elsewhere. Another example would be how a new candidate will assume the position of the President of the United States every fourth and sometimes eighth year. The word also makes reference to the traditional feast commemorating the Virgin Mary's assumption into heaven celebrated by certain denominations. These two definitions, as well as the common psychological significance of the word are not the purpose nor direction of my focus. It is in the areas of human contact and relationships which require more attention and much needed awareness.

## ELEMENTS OF ASSUMPTION

The principal definition of the word assumption I am targeting is based on how people think or what they believe regarding others on a daily basis. In my research, I found the idea to have many facets I never grasped before, which is another reason why it became so significant to me.

In its simplest form, it means to think, expect or believe something is true or is going to happen without absolute supporting evidence or proof. You are essentially taking for granted and grasping a thought, idea or opinion in your mind as accurate or factual based on insufficient information. It is this very part of our lives that gets us into so much trouble.

> We can't always fix what has happened in the past, but we can change things for our future.

Three components of assumption which stand out above the rest are thought, belief and expectation. Have you ever done something you were asked to do, only to later find out it was not what was requested of you? When a friend or family member told you a certain individual was a mean person, did you believe what they said, accepting it as truth? Have you ever been in dire need of help over a situation and expected your best friend or close relative to help you, just to end up frustrated and upset when they didn't? In each of these examples, we assumed something was one way but found it was not that way at all. We became a casualty of assumption, and it caused problems and grief.

I cannot count on my hands and feet how many times I have fallen victim to my own assumptions. Countless times, I thought someone said one thing, when they actually said another. I believed what others claimed and made decisions based on what I heard, instead of doing the research myself and calculating the costs before making reckless mistakes. I have placed expectations on people to perform certain things just to end up hurt, upset and disappointed. Because of my continuous assumptions, I have lived life hard, and I am still paying the price for some of those errors.

## TOO MUCH ASSUMPTION

Why do we assume so much in our lives? The first obvious reason is due to our upbringing and conditioning. Another is our level of trust in a particular situation or towards another individual, which can also stem from the way we were raised and the experiences we faced growing up. Sometimes we just place a great deal of hope in a situation, which drives us to assume it will turn out the way we expect.

I lived the first sixteen years of my childhood in an abusive home. Mentally and physically, I was beaten down. I experienced unusual physical punishments and, at times, was even slapped in the face for trivial reasons.

On occasion, I would be struck on the chest or legs while taking a ride in the car. I was repeatedly told I would amount to nothing in life and was useless. I grew up that way, and it became familiar. My mindset was programmed to assume life was like that. I knew nothing else.

*Knowing about assumption now can save you a lot of suffering in the future.*

After spending time in family institutions, I was later adopted into a new family. This was a completely different family, not only in race, but in what they believed and the way they were conditioned. They were a caring and kind family and accepted me with open arms. Yet, every time I did something wrong, I assumed I would experience the same type of punishments and reactions I had as a younger child. Moreover, I was especially jumpy when my new parents would raise their hands for whatever reason, or I would flinch if they made any sudden moves when sitting close to me. I took an extended period of time to realize the same consequences were not going to happen in this new setting, but the affects would remain present in my psyche for many years because it was what I was accustomed to. My trust level was very low. I remained encompassed by the fear until this new life started replacing it. I struggled for even longer with the belief I was worth something in this world. I admit, my insecurity about being insignificant tries to rear its ugly head on occasion, but I can only shift those insecurities by renewing my thinking on a daily basis, no matter what others may think. I will addressed the topic of renewed thinking later in this book.

## ASSUMPTION IS DESTRUCTIVE

Assumption can be incredibly destructive and, as earlier stated, can kill. It acts as a cancer or virus, continually growing if you are not conscious of it. If we don't understand how to detect and control it, we position ourselves to enter into stress, insecurities, hopelessness, despair and even paranoia, living a miserable life. A life full of these stressors can easily lead to strokes, heart attacks, and other medical complications, but it can also result in crime and murder. I am not implying that you or I would ever go to such extremes, but it does occur.

*Understanding how to detect and control assumption positions us to experience better relationships.*

One evening, I was watching a reality television show dealing with crime and investigation. Two men had been brutally shot and killed, one in the apartment and the other chased down a few blocks. It became quickly evident the two men were roommates. No forceful entry was apparent, and it was obvious whoever killed them was a friend, relative or acquaintance. Hours later, the detectives noticed there was a third roommate, and evidence pointed to him as the killer. The living roommate was swiftly apprehended and taken to a room for questioning. When the facts were presented to him, he promptly confessed to the crime. When asked what happened, he simply said he thought his roommates were intending to kill him, and he decided to kill them first. No one will ever know what really happened, but this man allowed assumption to take over his thoughts, causing him to commit murder. Many of us will never experience this form of devastation, but we may have had friendships, relationships and opportunities totally shattered because we allowed assumption to dictate the outcomes.

## AWARENESS TO ASSUMPTION

I am certain if you look into aspects of your life where something did not happen as expected, it may have simply been because of assumption. We can't always fix what has happened in the past, but we can certainly change things for our future. Merely being conscious of the negative impact assumption has in our daily lives will allow us to get back on track making less mistakes and experiencing fewer disappointments.

## REVIEW

Assumption is here to stay. It is an element of our human intellect, which is part of our rational and emotional thinking process, making us who we are based on our upbringing and conditioning. Unfortunately, when it involves our social life, it can become potentially dangerous. It is capable of ruining friendships and relationships and perhaps causing medical complications, crime or murder. It acts as a cancer or virus, constantlygrowingifwedon'tunderstandhowtoidentifyand control it.

Assumption means to think, expect or believe something to be true or probable without complete verification. Becoming mindful of the negative impact it can have will allow us to experience fewer frustrations and better relationships.

## AWARENESS IN THE FAMILY

Continue researching assumption, and do what you can to understand it further. The more you comprehend and develop an awareness of it, the quicker you can eliminate its potential to do harm.

CHAPTER 2

# WHAT ARE YOU HEARING?

**HOW MANY TIMES** have you been involved in a quarrel based on what someone said or did not say? Can you recall ever witnessing a dispute like that one? More than half of the arguments I've heard or been involved in had to do with someone not correctly hearing what the other person said. Some of these fights ended up in break-ups, and others resulted in individuals not speaking to each other for an extended period of time. I can only imagine how many relationships end daily as a result of assumption or how many people lose their jobs because they didn't do what was requested. I've even observed children not speaking to their parents for years because of a slight misunderstanding. If you are a previous victim of this form of assumption, I can genuinely relate with you. I'm confident you don't have to go through those heartaches again.

I classify this form of assumption as thought or opinion. In other words, it is your point of view on a matter, or your interpretation of what you say or what you hear. It is most commonly recognized by the statement, "I thought you said..." While raising three children, I have expanded my own analysis by classifying it as "selective hearing," which I'll discuss later. Someone can clearly say the same thing to two people, and both could interpret it differently. The reason for this can simply be the way a person has been conditioned. It is the way they see it through their own filter of reasoning. A good example of this can be seen in the word "cool". There is no uncertainty in anyone's mind that the word is cool, but one individual hears it as the common slang for nice, neat or awesome. The other only comprehends the word as a temperature slightly warmer than cold. This does not make either one of them wrong, but if you were to put both of them in the same room to speak to each other, they may have a hard time understanding what the other is saying because they lack a common point of view with certain words.

## TELEPHONE GAME

I remember a game I used to play with a very

interesting outcome. A group of people would sit or stand in a circle. One member of the group began the exercise by quietly whispering a short sentence into the ear of the person to their right. The person to their right then relayed the sentence to the next person to their right, and the exercise would continue until it had completely gone around the entire circle. The last person to receive the sentence would announce it out loud to the group. The first person who relayed the message would then reveal what they originally said to see how the sentence was changed throughout the exercise. One name for it is called "telephone." Not once do I recall the last individual repeating the exact sentence as the one who initiated it. We loved this game, but little did we know, this type of bad communication would end up hurting us or others with whom we came in contact.

## PARTNERSHIP

Partner relationships seem to be stricken the hardest by assumption. The principle reason is because two people from different upbringings come together into a relationship not knowing much about each other. As they spend more time getting acquainted, the relationship begins to grow. If either one of them are not aware of the issues with assumption, it can lead to problems.

I want to introduce you to John and Jane as an example. Jane is a career woman in the legal field. She is very independent and secure. Her childhood was above average, never needing anything and exceptionally educated, which has produced a very confident and outgoing woman. She is direct and specific. John is a travel agent with an average lifestyle. He did not attend college, but graduated from a travel academy and has been in the industry for over seven years. He is mostly timid but very compassionate, and he takes excellent care of his clients. One morning, they meet at a local gym. It is love at first sight. Their attraction for each other grows, and they fall in love. Because of their passion for one another, the little issues they have do not affect their growth as a couple. Happy and content, they get married and begin their wonderful life together as Mr. and Mrs. Smith.

> We have to change our mindset and retrain our thinking towards assumption.

Years later, they begin to notice problems in their relationship, yet nothing specific comes to mind. Everyday life is good, and their stress levels are moderate, barring some problems John is having at work with his boss. Frustration inhabits their household as they notice they are arguing a lot. They still love each other very much, but are slowly drifting apart as the issues they are having can't seem to be resolved.

## UNHAPPY COUPLE

One Wednesday morning, Jane says, "The case I've been working should rule in our favor today. I'll try and call you when it's over, but if you don't hear from me, I'll be celebrating with my colleagues over dinner and I'll be home later. I love you!"

John quickly replies, "Okay, good luck and I love you, too!"

He heads off to work. His mind is focused on a vital package deal he must have completed by first thing Friday morning. It is a corporate contract for some Account Executives representing an Ad firm who need to travel to New York for a Convention which is very important to the company. He has a few other projects he needs to complete but is confident he'll have it ready by the end of the day on Thursday. He goes about his usual day and heads home, excited to see his wife for a romantic evening.

As she expected, Jane succeeded in the verdict. It was a big case in her career, and she wanted to share it with her husband. Before she could call John, members of the firm approached her with congratulations, and they insisted in going out to celebrate. Knowing what she communicated to John, she eagerly accepted and enjoyed a pleasant dinner with her colleagues. It was a high moment in her life, and she wished her husband was there to enjoy it with her. A few hours later, she motioned her farewells and headed home. She was exhausted from a productive day and looked forward to sharing the news with her husband, lying in their comfortable bed for a good night's rest.

> *It is important what you do with anger and how you handle it.*

As she stepped through the front door, she noticed John sitting at the dining room table looking upset. Her excitement overlooked his displeasure, and she began to say hello and declare the great news.

John swiftly interrupted her, "Where have you been Jane?"

"I've been at work and out to dinner, like I told you. Why, what's wrong?" she replied.

"No." John said, "You told me you would call me before making any decisions. I've been sitting here for hours worried about you, and you haven't answered your cell."

"That is not what I said, John, and I apologize. I had my phone in my purse on vibrate and forgot to turn the ringer on after leaving the courthouse." Jane replied in a frustrated tone.

"Yes it is! You said you would call me after work. I know what you said!"

"I told you I would try to call you, but if you didn't hear from me, I would be out to dinner with my colleagues and would be home later."

"Admit it Jane. You just don't want to spend time with me!"

Confused, Jane replied, "What? Did I ever say that? I never said that!"

"Do you even love me?" continued John.

"You are assuming that!" Jane shouted.

Mr. and Mrs. Smith continue arguing for the next half hour over things which had nothing to do with the original topic. Old subjects resurface, and past mistakes re-emerged. Upset and hurt, they sleep in different rooms. The next morning, no word is uttered, but a peck for a kiss and a dismal, "Have a good day." to be polite.

## HANDLE ANGER QUICKLY

Before moving on, I'd like to promote a particular scripture from the bible referring to going to bed angry. If you look up Ephesians 4:26, Paul suggests that you do not let the sun go down on your anger. Anger itself is not the issue. Things can make us angry. Anger is part of life. What is important is what you do with the anger, and how you handle it. Having it bottled up within can only hurt others and destroy relationships. I go through stresses of life like anyone else, but I sleep very well at night because I do everything I can to resolve any anger issues I may have before my head hits the pillow. I have gone to bed angry before without confronting the matter and it was a restless night. Do what you can to handle any anger you have before the sun goes down and, if possible, right away. It will not only maintain and build better relationships, but it will be one less thing on your mind as you go to bed.

## ASSUMPTION IN THE WORK PLACE

Work relationships also fall victim to this level of assumption. Unfortunately, this can leave people jobless and unhappy with their careers if not attended to. Let's revisit John Smith. It is now Friday afternoon, and he is getting back from lunch to finalize his New York package and hand it over to Lisa when she arrives. Lisa Walker is a single mother of two children and the branch manager of the company. She is not the type of boss that hangs over her employees, but she expects the best from them and will not tolerate errors. She attended a marketing meeting with the company leaders the previous evening, which continued this morning from nine to twelve. Because it was mandatory for her to be present at the quarterly meetings, she turned the New York project over to John.

After the meeting, Lisa grabbed her cell phone to turn it on. She had it off since the night before because cell phones were prohibited in the meetings. The instant her service connected to the network, seven messages appeared on her home screen. She sensed some importance and decided to listen to them before going to lunch. By the third message, she immediately turned the car around and headed straight to the agency. Driving beyond the speed limit, she just as quickly pressed the speed dial of her phone to contact John, who was not answering. She left a message for him to return her call immediately and continued to redial. John was at lunch by this time. His daily custom was to turn off his cell during his break in order to enjoy his hour, uninterrupted by calls. Knowing this, Lisa continued to dial, hoping today was not the same case.

John was pleased with the work he put into the New York project. This cheerfulness prevented him from remembering to turn on his phone before walking through the agency doors. He was immediately confronted by Lisa, who has been frantically awaiting his arrival.

"What happened with the New York project? They were suppose to leave today!"

"What?" John asked confused. "What are you talking about? I thought you said it was due today and they were leaving first thing tomorrow morning."

Frustrated, Lisa replied, "That is not what I said, John! I specifically told you they were flying out Friday, so they could arrive that evening and be fresh for Saturday morning. I also asked you to contact them before the end of the day Thursday with the confirmation!"

Distraught, John replied, "I'm sorry. I did not hear you say that. I thought you said you would call them."

As a result of the New York project failing, the clients could not find any last minute flights out on Friday. They were able to get an early flight out Saturday morning, but they would spend the day tired from the trip. Lisa's agency lost them as a client. Due to the nature of the mistake and John's assumptive errors, he was immediately discharged from the company. Frustrated and disappointed, John returned home to another night of arguments. John lost his job, and if something did not change, he could lose the love of his life. Is it all his fault? I'll address that question in the next chapter.

## AWARENESS IN THE FAMILY

Parents and children have this same dilemma but usually not as extreme as the previous examples because they have grown together through life. Fortunately, most of these relationships don't end abruptly, but do cause anger, hurt and disappointment. Some may be minor, but if left unchecked it can escalate to bigger problems in the future. This is where "selective hearing" seems more prevalent. I define it as taking key words from a statement and forming your own opinion of what was said.

When it involves children, you have to understand it is a learning process from the time they are born. They not only have to learn the given language, but they have to comprehend it. As a parent, if you are aware of the dangers of assumption, you can train them from the beginning. It will not only help in your connection with them but also the relationships they establish in the future in every environment in which they come in contact. This is very beneficial to the child, unlike those of us that have lived for a while not recognizing it. We have to change our mindset and retrain our thinking.

## ASSUMPTION WAITING AT HOME

Lisa Walker has experienced a tough day. She lost an employee in the company she cared about and lost a key client. She folds up the pink slip she received from her manager for her responsibility in the account and takes a deep breath. As she slides out of her car, she is pleased it is Friday and tries to forget about it for the weekend. She glances at the front door of her home and generates a relieved grin. Unfortunately, Lisa has not read this book and is completely unaware of the impact assumption can have in her life. She soon finds out her weekend will not be as pleasant as she assumed.

Jordan immediately greets her mother with loving kindness. At fifteen, she has been given responsibilities sharing in the load of maintaining a clean home. She doesn't have as many chores as her brother, James, who turned seventeen last month. Lisa immediately notices nothing has been done, and she's entered a catastrophe. Dishes are piled in the sink, the cat litter is full and the trash is jam-packed.

"Where is James?" Lisa asks, covering her nose from the stench.

"He's at Ricks house." Jordan answers.

"What? I didn't say he could go over there!"

"Well, he said you did."

Displeased, Lisa escorts Jordan to the bedroom to check if it has been cleaned while grabbing the phone to call James.

Surprised to see the room ransacked, she asks, "Jordan, why is your room not clean, and why didn't you clean out the litter box like I told you?"

With puppy-dog eyes, Jordan answered, "James said I could do it tomorrow since he was going to do his chores tomorrow, too."

James answers the phone.

Without introduction, Lisa shouts, "Why are you at Rick's and why are your chores not done? And why did you tell Jordan she didn't have to do her chores?"

"I didn't say that Mom!" Jordan interrupts.

"You said I could spend the night at his house, and I thought I could do the chores when I got home in the morning," James explained.

"No, I didn't say that James! I said, I didn't see a problem with that if you did your chores!"

"I was going to do my chores. You didn't say I had to do them today."

"You know you're supposed to do your chores today. Come home now!"

## SELECTIVE HEARING

If you notice, everyone claimed what someone else said, yet none of them were correct. The example of "selective hearing" I want to point out is when James heard "...I don't see a problem with that..." and he left the rest of it out, assuming he could spend the night at Rick's. Jordan assumed she didn't have to do her chores today because James decided to do them the following day. Therefore in her mind, James told her she didn't have to do them today. Lisa assumed that James told Jordan not to do her chores at all. This example is a train wreck of assumption, which happens often in this household. James is forced to come home, not only to do his chores, but is placed on restriction for disobeying his mother. He takes it out on his sister, assuming she got him in trouble, but he is also upset at Lisa and locks himself in his room all weekend. Jordan is sad that her brother is upset with her and stays to herself throughout the weekend as well.

> Anger bottled up within us can only hurt others and destroy relationships.

## THE ASSUMPTION VIRUS

All of the individuals in the previous examples are victims of assumption. Imagine if we continued expanding from them. How many more people are unaware of the virus that consumes so many families, undetected? How many relationships have to continue suffering before we get control of it? This is the biggest arena for assumption I see in everyday living. From families and businesses to finances and health, we are surrounded by this plague. We can stop this today! In the next chapter, I'll suggest a straightforward and trouble-free resolution.

## REVIEW

What are you hearing when people speak to you? Countless arguments have to do with someone not correctly perceiving what the other person is saying, causing anger, hurt, and disappointment. This may result in breakups, divisions, or unemployment. It is frequently identified by the statement, "I thought you said..." Recognizing this primary form of assumption as the way we hear or interpret what others are saying will eliminate a lot of difficulties.

We all get angry at times. What we do with anger can either hurt us and others or it will build better relationships and alleviate restless nights.

## PERSONAL APPLICATION

Assumption can penetrate every area of life. Pay attention to conversations and try to observe when assumption shows up. The further you progress in identifying it, the better prepared you will be to confront and control it.

## SCRIPTURAL REFERENCES

Ephesians 4:26

CHAPTER 3

# THE POWER OF COMMUNICATION

**AS YOU BECOME** more conscious of assumption, don't think others around you will. You can bring it to their attention when it appears and discuss it, but they will need to develop with it just like the rest of us. Also, don't presume, as you begin controlling assumption in clarifying yourself and asking questions, the other party is on the same wavelength as you. It will take time to get better in this area and may take longer for others if they don't have the same understanding as you. It took my girlfriend and me over a month to fully acknowledge its importance and start putting new behaviors into practice. Because we discussed the issue and made a decision to work on it together, it was not long before we saw positive results is our relationship.

The same outcome is evident with my children. They not only understand what I say better, but they have a grasp on assumption and are applying it in their school environment.

## COMMUNICATION IS KEY

Communication is the number one key to controlling assumption. It is defined as transmitting or conveying information by speaking or writing. In a transmission, there is a sender and a receiver. An example of this would be two individuals passing a football in a game of catch. One person passes the ball, and the other one catches it. In order to enjoy the sport, the ball must be tossed back and forth. If you throw the ball to your friend, yet he does not pass it back, the game is over. You have to make sure your conversations are not purely monologues, but dialogues. Do not be the only one speaking or listening, otherwise your communication will be ineffective.

Just because you talk to one another does not mean you are successfully communicating. One person may pass the football, but the other one may not catch it. The individual throwing may have a weak arm, therefore it is not delivered far enough. He may have a strong arm and hurls it too extreme. Equally, the individual receiving the ball may not be prepared when it is tossed and may miss the catch. If he is ready and the ball is thrown perfectly, he may not grasp it because it slipped through his hands. They have to keep practicing in order to effectively play the game. The more they play, the better they become in sync with each other. Each one learns the others' weaknesses and strengths, and they begin to adjust to one another, resulting in a better and more enjoyable game of catch. The same principle needs to be applied when communicating with others. Every person you come in contact with will have a different method of delivering or receiving information. The more you spend time with that individual, the more you understand each other and develop in effective communication.

## THE LANGUAGE BARRIER

In order to develop successful communication, you must begin with the understanding that everyone is unique. In the United States, most of us speak English, but this does not necessarily mean we speak the same language. A perfect example of this would be with the word "woman", which is defined as a female human being. A person from one area of the country may use the phrase "lady." Another individual from a different part of the nation may use the term "gal." These may be familiar uses in their particular culture, but it may not be received well by others. The word "woman" could also be construed differently depending on its use. "You are a very beautiful woman" would ordinarily be received as a positive statement. "Get out of the way, woman" would commonly be acknowledged as negative or demeaning. "She is an interesting woman" could be received in a positive or negative manner. Over the years, the English language has become extremely convoluted and diverse. It has been polluted and congested with slang terminology, which makes it much tougher to truly understand each other. As long as we recognize this, we can be in a better position to correspond effectively and with less offense.

## THE TRANSMITTER

People are going to assume. They may get insulted by something you say. There is no real way around it. We live in a society where people shoot each other over a slight misunderstanding. We have become a generation overly sensitive and insecure, yet demanding respect. The best you can do is try to close the gap of assumption by keeping lines of communication open and simple.

When you speak with others, especially with someone you have never met, talk as directly as possible. An excellent scripture in the Bible that describes this form of clear-cut communication is found in the book of Matthew 5:37. The straightforward interpretation of this verse is to let your "yes" be yes and your "no" be no. Be specific and simple in your speech. Do your best to eliminate any slang and make it as plain as possible. This does not mean they will receive it correctly or not get offended, but you minimize its potential. Be prepared to clarify what you mean if asked. This also applies when giving directives or requests. Take it a step further by asking the person to repeat what you have asked to ensure you are both on the same page. If you start putting it into practice now, it will become natural later on in interactions.

> *Communication is the number one key to controlling assumption.*

We can sometimes be a bit too direct, which can also cause assumptions. I have been guilty of this numerous times, and it has caused problems in the past. I spoke the truth and was very forward, but was too insensitive.

I am not big on long meetings. I am more of a "doer." I do not feel it takes two, three or four hours to determine an objective and act on a plan. One afternoon, I was called into a major marketing meeting, which would be lead by the CEO. As Director of Media, I represented the Video Production Department and needed to be in the meeting for some announced changes. If you were not mentally prepared for these intense meetings, the CEO would go way over your head. He was a visionary, and he always knew exactly what he wanted and how to go about doing it.

Two hours later, the meeting was over, and the CEO left the conference room. I am an extensive note taker, because I want to ensure I understand all that is required, and I want to keep the information fresh before me. I was getting up to leave and activate the new objectives, when other members of the meeting began to plan some additional meetings concerning all that was covered previously. Already exhausted from a lengthy conference, I was surprised at what was going on.

I said, "Guys, we don't need another meeting! He gave his directives and gave you all your instructions. Go and do what he said! I am not going to another meeting."

I was very direct and blunt, but I was not their superior; they were my colleagues. I could have communicated the same thing in a more sensitive and respectful manner, saying, "Guys, I disagree in having another meeting. He was very clear with his directives and gave us specific instructions. I suggest we go and apply them to our departments, and if we need to meet later, I will be more than happy to do so. I need to go and meet with my staff. Contact me if you need anything." I still conveyed my opinion on the matter and was specific, but minimized any issues.

You may pass the ball perfectly, but it does not mean the receiver will catch it. Equally so, you may throw a bad or wobbly pass, yet the receiver catches it. You can only do your best in transmitting information. Doing your part does not always guarantee the receiver doing theirs.

## THE RECEIVER

In the sport of football, catching the ball in the right place wins games. If the quarterback continues to pass the ball to a receiver who repeatedly misses the catch, he will look for another receiver to toss it to. Once he finds the receiver who can consistently adjust to his throws and makes the catches, they will become a force to be reckoned with. The quarterback has not stopped throwing the ball nor changed the style in which he delivers it. He merely found a receiver that could not only catch it, but adjust to his method of throwing.

What you do on the receiving end of a transmission can make or break a conversation or relationship. This is where we are most vulnerable to assumption and where we need the most work.

Each person passes or conveys information differently. It is our responsibility to position ourselves to receive better and be prepared to adjust toward different methods of delivery. In short, do not be so quick to assume what someone is saying or get insulted when they state something you may not be accustomed to. An excellent scriptural reference is found in the book of James 1:19. He suggests to be quick to hear, slow to speak and slow to anger. Aside from the message James is delivering, if we apply this to our thought process and conversations, we minimize the potential for assumption.

## QUICK TO HEAR, SLOW TO SPEAK

Listen to what the other person is saying and allow them to finish. Do not be so quick to respond. I have been guilty of speaking right in the middle of another's sentence. A friend of mine would be talking, which brought up something in my head, and I would interrupt them so I could say what was on my mind. This can happen a lot in arguments. It immediately opens the door to assumption, especially for the other party. When you interrupt them, they may assume you are not interested in what they have to say. You continue doing this, and they reach a point where they do not want to talk to you anymore. Also, when you don't let someone finish, you only hear bits and pieces of what they have communicated, which opens the door for you to assume things you shouldn't. If you treat your conversations as if you are speaking through a walky-talky, you both complete your sentences, leaving less room for assumption.

## SLOW TO ANGER

Do not be so easily offended at what people say. Monica, one of my best friends, mentioned a great example of this. Using the preceding instance with the word woman, her boyfriend was having a conversation on the phone and was asked what he was doing.

He said, "I'm taking care of my lady," because she was feeling ill.

Instantly, Monica could have been offended and yelled, "That is rude! Don't call me a lady, it's demeaning!" It could have dreadfully started an argument. Instead, she asked him why he said it because she was raised with the understanding it was a humiliating remark. He was brought up differently and explained how "lady" is a form of nobility, and a woman who is refined like a goddess. Though Monica's culture perceives it as rude and insensitive, she confronted assumption and found her boyfriend classifying her as a woman of royalty. In the future, Phil may be more sensitive to her understanding of the word and use another, but if he were to say "lady" again, Monica would have a smile on her face because she knows his interpretation. She was slow to anger and communication dissolved conflict.

## MAKING ADJUSTMENTS

Evaluating the dilemma between John and Jane, most of us would instantly assume John to be at fault. Unfortunately, such a conclusion would place us in another area of assumption which involves judgment. We pass the blame too quickly, having insufficient evidence. I would suggest not judging based on who is wrong, but who needs to work on the problem. In order to successfully grow the relationship further, they both have to make some adjustments. I am a firm believer of the adage "It takes two to tango." An effort from both parties of a relationship is required to solve every problem. One individual may need to work harder than the other, but neither one of them are excused from participating.

John appears to have some other matters he needs to deal with. He seems to have some insecurity issues. With Jane's help, if he buckles down and works to manage assumption, his lack of confidence will become a minimal issue. We also notice how his mind can get too far ahead of him, which affects his present conversations. As Jane was communicating what she was doing for the day, he had his mind set on the New York project. He only heard "I'll call you...dinner...I'll be home...I love you." The first thing John should have done at this point was to say, "I'm sorry. I have this major project I'm working on, and I was thinking about it while you were talking. Can you repeat what you said?" Surely, he would have avoided confrontation between them later in the evening.

## PORTIONS OF INFORMATION

I can personally relate to John when it comes to hearing bits and pieces of what people are saying. I am on the computer for one reason or another about seventy-five percent of the day. I'm either surfing web sites, doing research, playing games or working on a video project. I get very focused on what I'm doing at any given moment. Having three children that seem to need something every fifteen minutes, I can fall victim to assumption very quickly. Unfortunately, if you don't recognize it as a parent, children may observe the conduct and take advantage of it. The next thing you know, one of your kids is gone, one is burning food in the kitchen and another has no idea what is going on. Now you have to deal with other issues, which could have been avoided if the communication lines were open.

I finally had to sit my children down one day and explain how I get concentrated on what I am doing. I asked them to get my attention first before asking me if they could do something or share how their day went. It was important to me for two fundamental reasons. I want my kids to not only feel like I care but to know they are significant to me. I want them to get my undivided attention when it comes to something they want to do or is important to them. Not only does it help prevent additional problems, but it can dramatically negate insecurities in becoming part of their lives. If you don't give your kids the attention they need, they will get it elsewhere. Attention seeking behavior outside the home could be very dangerous for them. As a result of communicating my concerns with them, we are much closer and assume less, which makes our days go so much smoother.

## JANE'S CASE

Jane has much better communication skills than John. She is constantly facing clients, lawyers and judges on a daily basis. She is incredibly clear and direct because one slip of the tongue could end up losing a case or worse. In her defense, she was very specific with John. Based on his reply, Jane simply assumed he heard her and went about her day.

At work, she requests that certain things be repeated back to her, ensuring they understand what she has communicated. Unfortunately, she does not do it as well in her own home. Throughout the years, she has established a relationship with the man she loves. Jane knows him better than anyone else and occasionally notices his mind wandering on to other things. She can use that knowledge to better communicate with John. In her case, she should have asked him if he heard her and possibly asked him to repeat what she said.

## THE STARE

Have you ever been speaking to someone and they seem to be looking right through you? It can get very frustrating. They may have something else on their mind or are not really interested in the subject you are covering. Most of us brush it off, assuming they are paying attention, or we choose not to confront the issue because we wish to keep drama at a minimum. For some, it may not be a big deal, and they move on. For others, it can lead to bigger matters later. By simply confronting it right away and bringing attention back to your conversation, you prevent any potential problems.

## BETTER RESULTS FOR THE SMITHS

If either one of the Smiths would have recognized the open door to assumption, their evening would have turned out wonderfully. Jane would have been able to share the great news of her win, and John would have been happy for her, sharing in the celebration. They would have enjoyed their evening together and possibly made passionate love. Finally, they would have benefited from a good night's rest. It is much more pleasant to enjoy life with the ones you love when the communication lines are open and assumptions are kept at bay. If Mr. and Mrs. Smith continue to uphold their awareness of assumption and communicate effectively, they will soon observe less arguments and stress in their household.

*Communication and confrontation dissolves conflict.*

Sadly, John still has an enormous dilemma to face the next day, and he is unaware of his impending unemployment. Lisa, his boss, is going to bed assuming he has taken care of the New York assignment, and their clients will be flying out first thing in the morning.

## COMMUNICATION AT WORK

Lisa and John have some assumption issues they need to deal with. Everything done on the job is imperative to the growth and reputation of a company. Even though it is my opinion, I believe if there is ever a concern between a boss and an employee, the employee must make the adjustment. The boss has the final authority and ultimate control on whether or not someone keeps their job. The employee must respect that authority and make the necessary changes. I am speaking of a proper work environment, of course. When it comes to overstepping your authority or some form of harassment, you are dealing with another matter entirely.

John was approached by Lisa with the New York project. She gave clear objectives and deadlines, but John misunderstood them. He assumed he knew what was required and headed off to start the project. The outcome for him was unemployment. All he had to do was take a few moments and confirm the information and deadline.

## CONFIRMATION

From Military to Ministry, I have had some very tough jobs. One wrong move, and many lives could have been affected. I quickly formed a habit I call reconfirmation. If my supervisor came to me with a duty or assignment, I not only wrote it down as they spoke, but I repeated it back to them. I always made it a point to have a pen and pad with me everywhere I went. This may have frustrated them at times, yet I was not only concerned for my security but also for the lives for which I was responsible. I simply did not want to get it wrong. If the meeting was cut short and I didn't have time to reconfirm it, I instantly typed it up in memo form and delivered or emailed it to my boss.

John Smith did not reconfirm what Lisa asked him to do. That was his responsibility, and it cost him his job. If he would have taken a few extra minutes to confirm everything, not only would the company have kept their customer but also increased their potential to add more clients, ultimately increasing revenue for the business.

## OUR LEADERS IN AUTHORITY

Fortunately, Lisa is not my boss, and unlike John, I get to confront her. She was just as accountable for the loss as John was. All she received was a pink slip. John got fired. She was the original account executive, yet John paid the ultimate price. She could have avoided all of this by doing one of two things. Along with the file, she could have attached a memo explaining what needed to be accomplished and when it had to be completed. Additionally, she could have asked him to repeat what she requested to make sure they were both on one accord.

I have witnessed some awful bosses in my lifetime. Their heads were too big for their own good. They took advantage of their authority and paraded their power everywhere they went. It is a shame that people have to work for individuals who flaunt their authority so they can feel better about themselves. What about the type of bosses that are weak and do not lead well, yet managed to get into a leadership position? They are just as tough to handle because you spend most of your time trying to understand them. Fortunately, they can be easier to deal with as long as you keep strict communication with them.

*As ignorance to the law is no excuse, so is assumption.*

The trouble with having a terrible and insecure supervisor is there is not much you can do about it. Ultimately, they are your authority, and you can either accept it or go elsewhere. If you stay, they need to be respected, and whatever you feel must not be spoken to your coworkers. You would just be opening assumption to flow through the work place and setting yourself up for trouble you don't need. Of course, if it involves some form of abuse, you should report that to the authorities and let them handle it.

I do have a suggestion for anyone in this predicament, and it is scripturally based. If you look up First Timothy 2:1-8, Paul encourages us to pray for our leaders in authority and to do it without anger, which is good in God's sight. God knows the heart of every individual. We don't see what is really going on in our leaders' hearts; God does. Who better to talk to than God about a problem you are experiencing? Not only will He deal with their heart, but he'll also show you what you can do to be a better employee. It does not hurt to pray for your leaders so pray for your supervisors, your political leaders and your President. We need as much peace as we can get in our lives.

## THE GOOD LEADER

Fortunately, Lisa is not a bad supervisor and has a sincere heart. She simply made a mistake. She needs to learn from this experience, become sensitive to the dangers of assumption, increase her communication skills by having her employees repeat what she's requested and, if at all possible, put it in writing. Many of us hate paperwork, but I love paper trails. Admittedly, a paper trail does cover my tail, but they also makes it very easy to understand and communicate. Furthermore, it provides a reference you can revisit, especially when you have more than one project to handle.

You have to understand, all people in authority, whether they are leaders, managers or parents, have a lot of responsibility. The best way I can describe it is as a parent. Prior to having children, all I had to be concerned about was myself and my future. It was all about me and what I could do to become successful in life. Three children later, I still have the big vision for my life and plans for success, except I also have included three more lives; I am responsible for their accomplishments. I not only have to think about all I have to do and complete on a given day; I have to equally think for each of my children within the same time span. It will be easier when they are on their own, but they will always be my responsibility as long as I am alive. It is the same with those in authority over your life. Simply become more sensitive to all they are accountable for, and do what you can to keep assumption at a minimum and communication at its highest priority.

## LISA'S FAMILY

Lisa is also an incredibly caring and loving mother. She has wonderful children who adore and respect her and are exceptional in school. Sadly, assumption is slowly creeping in and opening the door to further issues in the future. Her kids are still developing and may not discern what assumption is. I am promptly reminded of a scripture in the bible. In the book of Hosea 4:6, it clearly states how people are destroyed for lack of knowledge. This is evident with our legal system. Not knowing a certain law enforced in your area does not excuse you from ending up in jail if you break it. If you are speaking on your cell phone while driving in a district which considers it against the law, you can be pulled over and fined. The officer will not accept your lack of knowledge as an excuse for breaking the regulation. As ignorance to the law is no excuse, so is assumption.

By sitting the family down and discussing the hazards of assumption, Lisa educates her children and prevents further complications in the household. Furthermore, James and Jordan will experience a smoother adulthood. The verses in Proverbs 24:5-6 refer to strength and safety in knowledge and council. They will have strong and solid relationships, because they were taught not to assume.

## REVIEW

Don't think others around you are conscious of assumption. People are going to assume. We exist in a sensitive civilization where language is remarkably diverse, filled with slang expressions and anything can go wrong over a minor misunderstanding. Try to close the gap of assumption by keeping lines of communication open and simple.

Communication means to transmit or pass on information by speaking or writing and is the primary key to controlling assumption. A conversations is not a monologue, but a dialogue. Do not be the only one speaking or listening, otherwise your communication will be ineffective. Everyone is unique and has a different method of delivering or receiving information. Remember, just because you talk to one another does not mean you are successfully communicating.

As the one talking, speak as precisely as possible. Do your best to keep out any slang and make it as simple as possible. Be prepared to explain what you mean if asked. When giving instructions, request to have them repeated to ensure you are both on the same page.

What you do on the receiving end of a transmission can make or break a conversation or relationship. Position yourself to receive better and be prepared to adjust toward different methods of delivery. Do not be so quick to assume what someone is saying or get insulted when they state something you may not be accustomed to. Listen to what the other person is saying and allow them to finish. Be quick to hear, slow to speak and slow to anger.

Communication dissolves conflict. As ignorance to the law is no excuse, so is assumption.

## PERSONAL APPLICATION

Evaluate yourself. How do you speak to others? Do you receive information well, or do you get easily offended? Do you reconfirm instructions? Expand your knowledge by continuing your research in assumption and communication. Take what you learn and educate others, especially your family members. Make it your highest priority and put it into practice. It will soon become natural, and you will observe less arguments and stress in your life.

## SCRIPTURAL REFERENCES

James 1:19
1 Timothy 2:1-8
Hosea 4:6
Proverbs 24:5-6

## CHAPTER 4

# FLAWED BELIEFS

**HAVE YOU** ever believed what someone said, only to find out later it was not true? Have you said something, believing you were right, but later realized you were wrong? When you met someone attractive, did you believe they were "the one" and, before long, find out they were far from it? If someone tells you they love you, do you believe them? When others are having a conversation, do you believe they are talking about you?

Many people are quick to believe in the certainty of something without any verification. How many lives have been damaged because of what they assumed to be true? I believed what others said and made decisions based on what I heard. Moreover, I believed specific things were going to occur in my life based on what I assumed was going to happen. As a result, I lived a rough life filled with mistakes I would pay for later. If I knew about assumption earlier, I would have avoided a lot of hardship.

I am not speaking about the type of belief that connects us to faith in God or His Word, which is another topic altogether. I am referring to our over-confidence and swift acceptance of ideas and things people say, without knowing the facts. This is the next component of assumption we should not ignore.

## DEFINING BELIEF

My objective for this chapter is to help you to become further aware of this second element of assumption, called belief, which means to have confidence in or be persuaded into the reliability or existence of something to be true, without absolute proof or immediate evidence. In other words, you assume someone is telling the truth or something is obtainable. Likewise, you assume someone is incorrect or something is impossible. There are countless examples that would fill a library. The following illustrations are ones I have learned from the most.

## BELIEVING OTHERS

Many people make promises. Few keep them.

I have made countless mistakes assuming people were going to do what they said. I have lost a house, cars, marriages and a lot of money because I was weak and quickly believed what people stated. Much of my loss was due to my career decisions.

I was heavily involved in computers in High School. It was love at first sight! I learned everything I could about programming and wanted to build a career around it. I turned to the military. When speaking to the recruiter, I asked to be placed into computer training. My plan was to join the army for four years and use the G.I. Bill to go to college, continuing my education in the field. I was living in Georgia at the time and was sent to South Carolina for Basic Training. I was later transferred to Oklahoma for Advanced Individual Training (A.I.T.) where I would be taught my Military Occupational Specialty (M.O.S.), which would be computers.

*Do not be quick to accept things or what people say without knowing the facts.*

Three days into A.I.T., I realized the only computer training I would receive was a hand-help box, which had a few buttons to deliver coordinates to the Artillery Division directing where to fire their missiles. I was given the title "Fire Support Specialist" and reassigned to Alaska. I not only was sent from one hundred and fifteen degree weather to fifty below but ended up in an infantry unit marching numerous miles carrying a hundred pound backpack and wearing tennis rackets for shoes. I was devastated and alone.

Within a two year period, I lost my virginity, was married and divorced, released from the military with a Bad Conduct Discharge and sentenced to one year in prison. Unfortunately, my mistakes did not end there.

Throughout my career in video production, which has been well over eighteen years, I continued to make decisions based on what I was promised. Because I trusted what people pledged, I ended living beyond my means. I chose places to live based on how much money they said I would make and all the wonderful dreams they had for my future. I was too sensitive and ignorant, which resulted in bankruptcy and another failed marriage of fifteen years. Of course, there were other issues that caused bad results, but they all stemmed from believing in what others said. Knowing what I know now would have saved me a lot of suffering.

### BELIEVING YOURSELF

The next aspect of belief I have observed, is people thinking they are right. They assume they are always correct, and there is no one or nothing that will change their belief on a matter. It's their way or no way.

Sometimes it may be a simple error. Yet, often we have a point of view about something, and we later find out we were wrong.

When I was in my early twenties and living with my adopted parents, all I ever wanted was to be like my father. Being the son of a preacher, I would lock myself up in my room and record sermons as if I was standing on the pulpit. I would duplicate my dad's teachings and dreamed I would one day fill his shoes. Unfortunately, any time I would look at him and how remarkable he was, I felt incompetent. I thought there was no way I could ever come close to his greatness. Because of my insecurity, I never believed God wanted me to follow that path. No matter what other colossal men of God ever spoke over my life, they were wrong in my viewpoint.

It was not until my late thirties when I began accepting the unique gift God had placed in me. I wasted so many years trying to be someone else, searching to find my place in this world. I enjoyed working in the field of television and have fantastic memories. Yet, I continued to make mistake after mistake, doing what I thought I should be doing. I believed I was right, and assumption got the better of me.

Another trivial example of thinking I was right was when I would be in a discussion over a movie or show I previously watched. We would argue about what took place in a particular scene. I clearly believed I was right. When reviewing it again, I found I was wrong. This would be a very simple oversight, but it applies to countless areas of our life when we believe we are accurate. You risk becoming close-minded, which can result in being vulnerable to so much assumption.

## NEW FOUND PASSION

Fear and insecurity can be very dangerous in the area of assumption. If you don't work on those issues and become aware of them, you can waste years of your life doing something you were never suppose to do. I continued to be a victim of this type of assumption.

I was hired by my father as a producer, working on daily programs and commercials for him. I initially did not know anything about television. With my wild thinking and intense creativity, I would be able to bring something fresh to the department, while I would learn the ins and outs of producing.

I jumped in with both feet. I wanted to learn it all! I fell in love with the whole industry immediately. As a producer, I basically set things up and wrote scripts or outlines, while other team members like camera guys, editors and the audio department helped me make what I had described on paper into a final video project. I was so excited! I could actually take what was in my head and bring it to life on video. It was also the first time I began feeling I was worth something.

Unfortunately, I found myself always having to rely on others to get my work done. If I needed something filmed and the cameraman was not available, I had to wait. If I needed voice-over work or needed something edited, but they were not accessible, I could not move forward. At times it would affect my deadlines and I could face disciplinary actions.

With my true-found passion for television and my desire to be self-sufficient in getting my job done, I would show up as early as five in the morning and would stay as late as ten at night, so I could learn all that I could. I spent countless hours learning all the equipment and the intricate details of video editing. Of course in those days, there was no such thing as non-linear editing, though it was close around the corner. Everything was reel-to-reel. It was not long before I was able to produce and edit commercials and entire programs without any assistance.

> Let go of the past and decide to change it for a better future.

I grew to be incredibly valuable. Sadly, it had a draw-back that would eventually cause many problems. My direct supervisor began requiring me to film, create graphics and edit all of my work without a promotion or increase in salary. My hard work and dedication to learn became a thorn in my side.

One week, we had been given additional projects with unrealistic deadlines, which could have been avoided if my boss would have communicated the work-load we already had. He assumed the team could pull it off by taking advantage of my new skills and assigned the project to me. Even working over sixteen hours a day, I was over-loaded with assignments and did not get everything done in time.

My boss and I rarely got along because I would constantly give him a hard time about how he overworked us. He continued to place more responsibilities on the little staff he had and would not do anything himself to help us accomplish the work. I would confront the issues, but my colleagues would quietly evade them. I worked as hard as I could to help the department stay on track, while everyone else avoided the problems.

I heard my supervisor was going to go to my father and attempt get me fired because I did not meet my deadlines. I immediately grabbed all my paperwork and headed to my dad's house. It was late in the evening when we finished our conversation. He assured me I would not be fired, and he had my back. He would go in the next day and meet with my boss to get his story, handling the situation. Regrettably, even after he told me everything would be okay, the next decision I made cost me years of headaches.

## IMPULSIVE DECISION

I was young and just getting into the industry. Though my talent was growing rapidly, I had not developed my people skills in the work place. I knew I was weak in this area and felt my supervisor would handle it in a way that would make me look guilty. Because of this, I could not sleep all night. At four in the morning, I wrote a letter of resignation and drove it to my work, planting it under his door with a post-it stating, "You got what you wanted. Good luck on all your deadlines."

I returned home and shut the phones off. By four that afternoon, I sold most of what we had, purchased a hitch for our Eagle Talon sports car, connected a two-ton U-Haul trailer to the back, packed what we had left and began driving to Alaska with a three year old, a newborn and a pregnant wife. We arrived a week and a half later after stopping in Seattle for a few days. We began the process of starting our lives from scratch, not once contacting anyone for months.

I did not believe my dad. I assumed I would get fired no matter what he said. My trust level and my personal fears made me believe I would be the one that looked bad and would be to blame. I didn't want to be there when it happened, and it affected my relationship with my father. Mistakes like this one continued to affect my connection with him years later. This is just another case of how destructive assumption can be when we allow it to affect the decisions we make.

## GETTING ON THE "D"!

The previous accounts were major turning points in my life. My position in what I believed or assumed to be true, resulted in numerous challenges throughout the years. The next few illustrations are more trivial, yet can grow to bigger issues later on if not detected.

My girlfriend and I joke together a lot. It is an integral part of our relationship. It keeps things between us fresh and fun. Sometimes we tend to go just a tad bit too far, and one of us freeze and immediately get on the defense. We relate to it as "Getting on the D." In essence, one of us may utter something immediately making the other suspicious about what was said, and we become self-protective. Though we were poking fun, it may bring up old wounds and instantly upset one of us. If we were not mature in our relationship, it could develop into a big argument and potentially ruin our bond.

This can happen in disagreements frequently.

John, in an earlier chapter, is a prime illustration of getting cynical. Him and his wife Jane were arguing about a phone call when he introduced an entirely different subject concerning whether his wife wanted to spend time with him or not. He even went as far as questioning her love for him. We have to be very careful not to assume things beyond the topic at hand.

## ASSUMPTION CAN LEAD TO PARANOIA

It was tough working in a ministry as a Pastor's son. I was very different, but had to be extremely careful because I represented him and what he stood for. The biggest challenge I faced was thinking people were always talking about me. I believed no one liked me. I would constantly walk around paranoid, which affected my attitude towards people for years. Because of this, I became very distant from not only my coworkers but my family and friends for years.

## AN IMPROVED OUTLOOK

As you have witnessed, there are countless ways we can get into big trouble by believing something to be true when it is not. I am certain you have fallen victim to this form of assumption in one way or another. It has caused some pain and disappointments, but let go of the past; take what you have learned and decide to change it now for a better future.

## REVIEW

We need to become aware of this second element of assumption, called belief. Many lives have been damaged because of what they assumed to be true without immediate evidence. We may be too quick to believe what others say. We assume someone is telling the truth or something is obtainable. Similarly, they assume someone is incorrect or something is impossible.

Making career decisions based on what family, friends or recruiters promise can result in much loss. Also, making choices based on what you assume, is the right way to go and can affect many wasted years doing something you were never meant to do.

Be careful not to get defensive when involved in a discussion, even if you are joking around, and do not allow paranoia to consume you, believing others are speaking about you. It is not worth the trouble it can cause further down the road.

## PERSONAL APPLICATION

Look back into your past and see where you may have done something based on believing someone or some thing. Do not enter into guilt or regret. Learn from it, as well as my past mistakes, and turn to the next chapter.

I'll suggest ways you can prevent it from happening again in your future.

## CHAPTER 5

# DO YOUR RESEARCH

**AS I STATED** in the Introduction, I have excelled in the arena of mistakes throughout my lifetime. This does not mean I have had a horrible life. I was simply a casualty of much assumption due to my lack of understanding and awareness of it. There are numerous changes I would make if I were to do it all over again. It is a thought that has crossed most of our minds at one point or another. At the end of the day, if I had the opportunity to go back in time, I would have to decline the offer.

One thing I am is very happy. Even in the midst of tribulation, I find much joy in what I am doing. I love life and the opportunities it brings. Every morning I wake up, it is a fresh day. It is a chance to do better than the last. It may be rough at times, but I have more blessings to count than past mistakes. What do you do when you fall down? You get back up and try again!

Two powerful scriptures in the bible that keep me going daily are found in Romans 8:18, 34-39 and Philippians 3:13-14. I don't need to live in guilt and condemnation. There is nothing that can separate me from the love of Christ. He has made me more than a conqueror. I continue to reach, stretch and press to bigger and better things and the calling God has on my life. The best thing I can do is to share my mistakes with you, so you can learn from them. If you do mess up, get back on your feet and try again. Staying down and giving up are the worst things we can do.

## TAKE YOUR TIME

As you witnessed in the previous chapter, I made a lot of errors and impulsive decisions based on what I believed. It resulted in positioning myself out of the will of God many times but taught me some valuable lessons. Along with communication, doing your research will amplify your battle against assumption. We need to slow down, take the time to evaluate what has been said and calculate the cost before coming to a conclusion.

We live in a society wanting everything now. We recognize it by the term "microwave world." We see someone succeed, and we try and duplicate them, not understanding the steps it took to get there. We view an infomercial promoting a "product of the century," and we are swift to believe it, grabbing our credit card, not understanding the business of direct response marketing. Many people have lost their savings by investing in "get rich" schemes because the spokesman was so convincing, and it appeared to be a fool-proof system. Moreover, groups of people have died believing in a concept an individual proclaimed was sent by God. If we simply slow down and do our research, we can avoid so many problems.

## UTILIZE YOUR PARENTS

When I joined the military, I thought I had it made. I was in such a hurry to get out of the house. I was going to be able to do what I wanted and no longer had to follow my parent's rules. Three days after high school graduation, I was in a plane on my way to Basic Training. In less than two years, I was calling my parents telling them I was in jail.

The internet was not that big in those days, but there were plenty of resources to get solid information about the field for which I signed up. I could have easily sat down with my parents and discussed it with them.

It would have also given us the opportunity to talk about all the options I had available. If you are a teenager, use the greatest resource you have available: your parents. Overall, they are the ones that care for you the most. They have lived longer than you and have learned from mistakes they made in the past. They are on your side. Use them to your advantage, and be open-minded. The more extra time you spend communicating with them and allowing them to help you see everything clearly, the more time you will save having to get out of trouble.

## MORE COUNCIL

I came into my new family with a lot of fear and distrust because of my childhood upbringing. My adopted parents loved me and wanted the best for my life. My father gave me many opportunities, but my lack of trust kept disappointing him. If I would have been his natural son, things would have been different, and I would have made better decisions. Unfortunately, he took me in as a troubled and hard-headed teen, which made it tough for the ones that loved me the most.

I had the best research available to me: my family. Use yours to your advantage. Do not make decisions without communicating with them. They can present scenarios and challenges, so you can better plan for them and calculate the cost. Use your friends as well. The more people you have involved in your decision making, especially when it has to do with your career decisions, the better. As I pointed out in an earlier chapter, in the midst of council there is strength and security (Proverbs 24:5-6).

*There is always room to learn more and understand things better.*

## LEGAL ADVICE

When offered a job opportunity, make sure you not only research the company, but you get everything you are promised in writing before you sign any contracts. I also suggest, you invest the funds to have a lawyer review all the paperwork. The amount of money and time you spend getting legal guidance is nothing compared to the hardships you could face later on. Do not be tempted to neglect this advice even if it is a family member or friend offering you the opportunity. They may have every intention to do what they say, but not having it in writing and making decisions based on their promises can get you into trouble you do not need, possibly affecting your relationship as well. Sometimes we mix personal relationships with business, which can lead to more assumptions. Keep them separate at all cost.

## STAY FOCUSED

We can become very vulnerable in desperate times. When we experience some form of loss, we can be subject to believing more than we should. When we are weak and down, everything looks better from that position. Trials will come; it is a part of life and unavoidable. Jesus confirms this in the book of John 16:33. He also states to be cheerful because he has overcome the world. Stay positive when facing troubled times. Know God has your back and remain peaceful and focused. Remember, this is where we can open the floodgates of assumption, believing everything people say, dropping our guard and neglecting communication and research.

## YOU HAVE BEEN RESEARCHED

Countless marketing and advertising campaigns are designed to capitalize on our fears and weaknesses. The primary thing you need to know is they have done the research on you. They have spent years and millions of dollars on reports and analyses on how consumers react to certain phrases and products. We seek to make our lives simpler and more efficient, and we want it fast; they know it.

If they have spent all their time and money

examining you, shouldn't you do the same? Fortunately, tougher regulations are forthcoming by the Federal Trade Commission, but this still does not excuse us from doing our own research. I highly suggest not making any serious decisions when you are in the middle of a tough time.

## MOTIVATIONAL SPEAKERS

I cannot go without touching on the subject of speakers to some degree. Whether they are motivational speakers, lecturers or ministers, they pronounce a lot of wonderful things, and we can instantly believe them because they make us feel good at the moment. There are numerous great men and women who are sincere in their causes and beliefs. There are tremendous people of God who speak the truth according to the scriptures. Again, this does not excuse us from taking notes and reconfirming what they say.

As history has shown, cults have been built on the foundation of assumption and misinterpretation. How many "religious" groups can you remember that ended in death? One would be too many. As I covered earlier, assumption can kill. Do not just believe them because you felt good and the environment was so majestic, especially when visiting as a guest. Take what you heard home and study it yourself.

## FIND A CHURCH

I don't suggest going from one church to another or listening to a lot of different ministers throughoutthecountry,evenontelevision.Hearingthatmuch variety can put too many diverse thought patterns in your mind and spirit, which can lead to confusion. They all have opinions or their own interpretations. My advice is to tread lightly and confirm everything that has been spoken. Find a local pastor you relate to the most who teaches from the scriptures. Again, do your research. Furthermore, only spend time listening to ministers they are directly under.

*Do not be close-minded and un-teachable.*

I expect you to take everything I mention in this book and do your research as well. Again, my objective is to simply make you aware that assumption is out there, everywhere we turn, and if you are at least conscious of it and you can use some of my suggestions to make your life smoother, I have accomplished my mission. Research it for yourself and come to your own conclusions. I am only interested in you experiencing less difficulties in life and being less of a victim to assumption; there is enough evil in a day.

## THE INTERNET

The greatest asset we have for doing research is the internet. Whether it is an individual or company you want to find out about, you'll find it on the web. You no longer need mass libraries of dictionaries, references and concordances. The net is full of them. You can find reports, analysis and masses of information. Before making any decision that will affect your future, use the world wide web to help you to do your research and make a quality decision.

## ASK GOD FOR DIRECTION

Trust and believe the Spirit of God that is in you. Matthew 6:32-34 in the bible states to seek God first, because he knows exactly what you need. When doing all your research, He is the one that will give you the ultimate peace in any given situation (Philippians 4:7).

When you wake up in the morning, take time to study His Word, even if it is only for fifteen minutes; it will never be time wasted. Spend a moment communicating with Him in prayer and ask Him to lead you through the day, guiding you in all your decisions. Place your confidence in God, and he will guide you and help you not to be so quick to believe everything you hear (1 John 5: 13-15).

## BE TEACHABLE

Finally, do not be so close-minded and un-teachable. No matter how smart you are, how much schooling you have received or how scripturally versed you are, there is always room to learn more and understand things better. I have witnessed some well educated people with little common sense. You would be amazed what you can learn from people with street-smarts. No one can be right one hundred percent of the time. We are human. We make mistakes and bad judgment calls. I was hard-headed most of my life, thinking things could only be done one way. Though I have always been teachable, I allowed what I believed to be true and the right way to do things to cloud my judgement. As you have heard, my way was not always the best.

Renew your mind with God's Word every day. Open your spirit to all God has to offer. God loves you beyond your wildest imagination. He wants the best for you every day. Spend as much personal time with Him as you can. You will soon find out how much He can help you on the road to less assumption and greater days.

## REVIEW

What do you do when you fall down? You get back up and try again! You don't need to live in guilt and condemnation. It will make you weak and more susceptible to the dangers of assumption.

Slow down, take the time to evaluate what has been said and calculate the cost before making any conclusion. If we do our research, we can avoid so many problems. Your family is the greatest resource you have available for council, especially your parents. They are on your side. The time you spend communicating with them and allowing them to help you see things clearly, will save years of difficulties.

When offered a job opportunity or business proposition, make sure you not only research the company but you get everything in writing. Seek legal counsel to review all the paperwork. The amount of money and time you spend getting legal guidance is nothing compared to the hardships you could face later on. The best asset we have for doing research is the internet. Before making any decision that will affect your future, use the world wide web to help you make a quality decision.

Just because a motivational speaker or minister

sounds powerful and has a large audience, we are not excused from taking notes and reconfirming what they say. Take what you heard home and study it yourself. Do not be close-minded and un-teachable. There is always room to learn more and better understand things.

Trust and believe the Spirit of God that is in you. He is the one that will give you peace in any situation. Take time to study His Word and speak with Him in prayer. Ask Him to lead you through the day and to guide you in all your decisions. Place your confidence in God because He has your back.

## PERSONAL APPLICATION

Take all your past mistakes and throw them in the trash. Because of the blood of Jesus, God's love is the only true, unconditional love. Ask him to forgive your faults and to help you become more sensitive to the hazards of assumption.

## SCRIPTURAL REFERENCES

Romans 8:18, 34-39

Matthew 6:32-34

Philippians 3:13-14

Philippians 4:7

Proverbs 24:5-6

1 John 5: 13-15

John 16:33

CHAPTER 6

# FALSE EXPECTATIONS

**THE LAST ELEMENT** of assumption I want to cover is in the area of expectations. They have a great impact on our feelings, conduct, and most significantly, our performance. If we are not careful, this component of assumption can set us up to be disappointed, discouraged and unmotivated, which can result in despair, hopelessness, distrust and doubt. How many of your relationships have gone badly because of different expectations? How much money have you lost because of high expectations? Have you had to fix a problem because you worked with unrealistic expectations? If we can control this final hurdle of assumption, we can experience breakthroughs in numerous areas of our life.

## DEFINING EXPECTATION

The word expectation means to confidently anticipate or look forward to something likely to occur. Most of us relate to it as a mental picture of the future. We may see trouble coming or perceive something good is going to happen. It also applies to something we may consider as due or owed to us based on what we have done or are a part of.

We start getting into trouble when we initiate high or false expectations towards people or things. We begin to assume too much and enter into mistaken, superficial, inaccurate or misleading expectations.

## DIFFERENT EXPECTATIONS

Years ago, my biological mother and I were involved in an argument concerning certain expectations she placed on me. My wife and I were going through some tough challenges in our marriage, and I was spending most of my time raising the children alone, trying to keep the family together. Additionally, I was working full-time on video projects from my home office, which kept my days incredibly demanding. I did not get out of the house much, except to deliver tapes or buy groceries. We lived about an hour apart and seldom saw each other because of my difficult schedule.

Throughout the year, she would send us birthday cards and letters and would occasionally call to see how the kids were doing. I would get in touch with her when I could and frequently reminded the kids to call their family members to maintain contact with them. I assumed they were doing so.

Whenever she would call, she would confront me asking why none of us thanked her for the cards she sent or why we would not call or come and visit her. She criticized how much she missed her grandchildren and how upset she was that I would not bring them over to see her. We did not have a single conversation without her complaining about something one of us did not do.

> Do not place unrealistic expectations on family members, friends or coworkers.

What I could not understand was how she would rant and rave about how much she missed the kids and how sad she was it had been so long since she had seen them, but she would never take the initiative to drive out to see them herself. She placed all the responsibility on me and expected us to come to her.

I did not get along with my in-laws much, but I certainly respected them for the love they expressed towards the children. They did not care if we were busy or in the middle of something. If they missed their grandkids and wanted to see them, they made it a point to stop over, half of the time, unannounced. Despite our differences, I admired the fact they never had an excuse not to visit.

In the midst of another confrontation with my mother, frustrated and overwhelmed, I told her I was tired of her complaining and I was done arguing. I had not communicated to her the issues I was facing, but she assumed we were the ones that had to initiate the visits. I did not feel it was necessary to share the information with her and said if she truly missed her grandchildren, she would find the time to come and see them. I informed her that we would no longer be contacting her and not to expect anything from us again. I believed if she did not expect it, she would appreciate us more, and we would not have these types of arguments again. I also figured she would eventually come and see the children. Sadly, we did not speak or see each other for many years later. We were both wrong in this situation, and because we had different expectations, our relationship was affected for quite some time.

## HIGH EXPECTATIONS

Throughout my career in ministry, I placed considerable expectations on pastors of churches. Nine years ago, I launched a production company that produced commercials and television programs for various customers. The majority of my client-base was ministries. I specialized in post-production graphics and effects, and most of the profits resulted from creating 3D animated intros for their television broadcasts.

Negotiations and contracts were simple. We would set-up a budget, and I would require a fifty percent deposit to begin the project. I would request their video and a copy of their vision, or mission statement. I reviewed everything, negotiated music and began designing the opening based on what we agreed upon. Once the project was completed, they would send the balance of the invoice, and I would deliver the final work in their specified format.

> Expectations have a great impact on our feelings, conduct, and our performance.

Being ministers, I placed a higher trust on their word. If they stated they were interested in contracting me to work, I believed them and expected to have money coming in that month. On a few occasions, I made financial decisions that caused problems because I assumed I had a job. For example, a client confirmed he was interested and would get his people to start preparing a package to send me. Due to the nature of the project and expecting to have the funds available shortly, I spent a sizable amount of money upgrading my animation software. Shortly after installing it into my system, I received a call from the minister saying he would not be able to contract me for the job. The reason is not important, but because I expected to have this contract, I ended up in a financial bind. Because of assumption, I spent the next three months trying to catch up on my mortgage, coming very close to losing my house.

I continued making bad decisions based on assumptions certain things would occur, ultimately causing me to go out of business shortly after the 9/11 incident. My expectations were not viable, and my actions resulted in difficulty for myself and my family.

## UNREALISTIC EXPECTATIONS

Sometimes we place unrealistic expectations on family members, friends or coworkers. For instance, if a woman hires her mother or someone hires his best friend but expectations are not communicated clearly, these relationships could end in disaster. The mother may expect special treatment and assume that her daughter will support her over others because they are family. The daughter is going to expect that her mother respects her as her boss and assume she will not try to take advantage of their relationship. The best friend may expect leniency and favor, when his friend assumes he will be grateful for the opportunity and work harder than anyone else.

It took years for me to understand the difference between work and home with my father. I understood he needed to have my respect and to keep personal issues out of the work environment. The part that was tough was when we would be visiting at one of our homes, and I could not have any conversations about work. We had differences of opinion in this area, but if I wanted to work for him, I had to go by his policy. It is important not to assume certain expectations when they are not there. I have witnessed relationships destroyed because expectations were too high or unrealistic.

## REVIEW

Expectations have a great impact on our feelings, conduct, and most significantly, our performance. If we are not careful, this component of assumption can set us up to be disappointed, discouraged and unmotivated, which can result in despair, hopelessness, distrust and doubt.

Expectation means to look forward to something likely to occur, to regard something as likely to happen. It as a mental picture of the future. We begin experiencing problems when we start placing high or false expectations on people or things.

## PERSONAL APPLICATION

Think of examples where you may have placed unmerited expectations and evaluate if it involved an assumption on your part. In the next chapter, I will suggest ways to avoid this final element in our fight against assumption.

## CHAPTER 7

# BE REALISTIC IN YOUR EXPECTATIONS

**EVERY DAY WE FACE** three basic forms of expectation: our personal expectations, what we expect from others and what is expected of us. These stem from what we have been taught, our past experiences and what we set our mind to. They can either drive us forward to great accomplishments and relationships, or they can drag us down to discouragement and hopelessness.

It is important to reevaluate your own individual expectations, ensuring they are realistic and aligned towards the goals we are trying to accomplish. It is equally vital to cancel out all assumed expectations we have towards others and their expectations of us. The following suggestions will assist you in lessening the impact assumption can have in your life by effectively dealing with false expectations.

## EXPECT THE WORST,
## HOPE FOR THE BEST?

We must evaluate our personal expectations before we can work on the others'. We cannot go beyond ourselves before dealing with what is on the inside of us. For the longest time, my expectations got me in a lot of trouble. I needed to find a way to protect myself from the difficulties I was facing.

As far back as I can remember, I heard people use the statement, "Expect the worst and hope for the best!" It was very catchy, and I liked it. It was a great way for me to guard myself from any hurt. If something went wrong, it was not a big deal because it was anticipated anyway. When things went right, I was happy because I did not set myself up for disappointment and my hope came to pass.

I started noticing more challenging things happening. Of course, I always expected the worst, so while it wasn't shocking, I was getting depressed because my life felt useless and unfulfilled. Having bad expectations and meditating on them will only lead you to hopelessness, in effect, canceling out "hoping for the best." If you follow the first part of that statement, you will never get to the last part. Negative thinking only produces negative results. What you think and what you expect are what will come to pass. If you have ever lived by the above statement, stop now, it is unhealthy, unwise and you are only going to reap negative results.

## EXPECT NOTHING, APPRECIATE EVERYTHING?

A few years ago, I came up with a new phrase, "Expect nothing, appreciate everything." I could still protect myself, and I did not have to manifest any bad thoughts. Unfortunately, I found this was not working either. I observed less negative thinking, but I also recognized my life was stagnant. Though it was not getting worse, it definitely was not moving me forward. When good things happened, I appreciated them a lot more than I used to, but I needed more.

> *What you think and what you expect is what will come to pass.*

When I began researching the subject on assumption and started making the changes in my daily life, I realized I did not have to protect myself anymore. I confronted it, communicated better and changed the way I thought about handling my expectations. As a result, my thinking is more positive, my days have improved and my relationships are stronger.

## EXPECT GOD'S BEST!

I now live by one expectation only. I place my expectations in God and nothing more. I recommend you do the same. He has a perfect plan for every one of us. In the book of Jeremiah 29:11, we see that God has thoughts of peace and an expected end that is good. For a long time, I continued to place expectations on myself that were unrealistic. I became a person I was not familiar with. I constantly beat myself up trying to be someone I thought I was supposed to be.

Just as we have to correspond with others, we cannot forget the one we have to communicate with the most, God. I set my mind to believe what God wants for me and that is His best. As it states in Philippians 4:6 in His Word, I bring all my issues and questions to God. I thank Him for what He has done and what He is continually doing in my life. Because I go to Him when it comes to my personal expectations, I can be confident that He hears me, and I will receive His guidance, as we see in 1 John 5:15. Do not place your expectations in people or things, but place them in God and trust He will direct your path. As a result, you will not be disappointed.

Do not allow your past mistakes to get in the way of God's best. Do not let fear of failing keep you from pressing forward. God wants you to succeed and have a healthy and wealthy existence. That is His will for you. Receive His blessing on your life, place your expectations on Him and His Word and do not let anything get in your way, including assumption, or make you lose focus.

## OTHERS' EXPECTATIONS

Not only did I have a tough time with my personal perceptions, but keeping up with the expectations others had of me as well. I tried for so long to meet other's expectations. Because I was so focused in fulfilling them, I ended up being someone I was not. It kept me unhappy and down.

Unless it is communicated and agreed upon, it does not matter what others expect of you. Do not let it bother you. Do what you know is right and do the best you can to live according to God's Word, Trust He will confront you when you stray from His path (Proverbs 3:6). If you have failed in the past, others may see it and assume you will fail again. Spending time trying to override their low expectations of you will only cause you to feel defeated. The good news is what they think should not affect you. Remember, it is what you think in your mind that matters.

You can also get in a bind when people see you succeed. They end up placing high and unrealistic expectations in you because you have a history of accomplishments. Then you may spend extra time trying to keep up with what they assume you should be achieving, which could stress you out and possibly cause you to slip up and fall short of their expectations. It is not worth the tension and anxiety it can bring.

Most of us are much tougher on ourselves than we should be. When it comes to achieving goals, we push ourselves to be the best. If we fall short in a task or we do not like something about ourselves, we become frustrated. I am a perfectionist, especially when it comes to something I have passion for or when I am doing something I believe God has directed me to do. If the slightest thing goes wrong, I tend to beat myself up over it because I expect to accomplish everything with excellence. No one needs the additional pressure from others to make it worse.

## OCCUPATIONAL EXPECTATIONS

Expectations from one person can be quite different from those of another. When it involves work or relationships, they must be clearly communicated and agreed upon. When I worked as Director of Media, I kept expectations to a minimum and ensured lines of communication were solid. We agreed on the concept,

"You make me look good, and I make you look good." No false promises were made, and we agreed to make sure everything was in writing. We did not leave room for any assumptions. My tenure went very smoothly, even when challenges arose, because we maintained valuable communication.

We all have different ways of effectively communicating. Some people do better when having extensive discussions or meetings, verbally making things clear. I prefer to have it in a written form because I can go back to it as a reference, and it keeps me from spending too much time discussing and not enough being productive. When meetings would occur, I made it a point to take notes and sent them in memo form to confirm what was addressed. Whichever way you work best, make sure you do not leave any room for assumptions or superficial expectations.

*Do not let fear of failing to keep you from pressing forward.*

I highly recommend you get all stipulations and agreements in writing if you are offered a job with a company which is making certain guarantees and benefits. For example, if they offer a salary and a percentage of commission, it is imperative for you to make sure the offer is not only documented, but adhered to the first month you are there. If you do not confirm it, you can end up operating with uncertain expectations and making improper decisions for your future, which could result in financial hardships and discouragement. As I stated before, it would be additionally beneficial if you had a legal professional review the documents prior to accepting employment. When everything is clear, realistic and in writing, you can live and work with a lot less worry and stress.

## PARTNER EXPECTATIONS

Because we have been raised differently, our expectations vary. For instance, I open doors for women, whether it involves entering a building or unlocking a car door. Some women expect that as well, but others may not. If you are out on a date, the man may be expected to pay the bill. If you are in a relationship, occasional gifts may be expected.

It is important to immediately communicate each other's expectations up front. Unlike in a work environment, having it in writing is not necessary, though I have witnessed some relationships that go to that extent. Whatever works for you, do it. Unless you come together and clear the lines of communication, assumed expectations can run rampant, and the relationship will not last.

If you are currently in a relationship, it would be a good idea for both of you to revisit each other's expectations and close the door to any lingering assumptions. My girlfriend and I try to do it as often as we can, along with other areas I have discussed. It not only keeps our relationship fresh, but trouble free.

## FAMILY EXPECTATIONS

Expectations within the family unit can cause a lot of problems if not handled correctly. Parents have certain expectations of their children and vice-versa. How you handle it in your home is up to you as long as you effectively communicate your expectations, and you stray from creating unrealistic or false assumptions.

The expectations my kids and I have for each other are extremely sound and unquestionable. I frequently sit down to reconfirm with them. On occasion, there may be some new developments or adjustments that need to be made, but the core issues are always unwavering.

There are definite responsibilities they must perform living under my guidance, such as homework and chores. I expect them to keep lines of communication open when they have personal issues or challenges arise. It not only helps to keep the household in order, but it trains them to be responsible in preparation for their future. They understand I expect them to do their best and strive to do what they believe God places in their spirits. If they make mistakes, they are to never quit and to endeavor to be the best they can be. They have made it very clear they will not give up on me and will continue to pray and trust in God I will make the best decisions I can for the family.

My children have no doubts in their hearts my love for them is unconditional. It may be tough for some people to understand, but there is nothing they will ever do which will cause me to desert them or tear them down. They are confident in the fact I will always be there for them no matter what happens. Any one of them can come to me when they need help without feeling uncomfortable. If I have any resources available to assist them, whether it is to advance their dreams or get them out of a jam, I will help them, even if they do not ask for it. They should not have to. I am their father and my thoughts of them are good and unshakeable. I pray for them daily, and my words about them will always be positive. They do not have to qualify for my love, and I have made it up in my mind, whatever they chose, they will never fail me. I place my expectations and trust in God and His Word. I follow His example based on Deuteronomy 31:6 in the bible. Because they understand my commitment to them, they know they can accomplish anything in life, and I will be right there to support them.

It goes without saying they will slip-up. I would not be a good father if I did not confront and correct them when they do something wrong. My children understand there may be times when they disappoint me and do things that I disagree with, but they will not be left feeling incompetent or hopeless. There are far better ways to talk to your children without making them feel unintelligent and ineffective. Of course, I've raised them from birth, and it makes a big difference when you coach them from the beginning. I did not wait until they became teens but started the day they were born (Proverbs 22:6). They are aware of the destructive power of assumption and have learned the basic principles to control it. That knowledge alone will help them be more successful in life.

## CLEAR ALL DOUBTS

If you are ever hesitant as to what someone expects from you, ask for feedback. Whether you agree or not, you will at least be aware of it and can deal with it, void of any assumptions. Managing expectations is essential, and anything you can do to clear them up will result in fewer misunderstandings.

It is important not to have inaccurate, unrealistic or

extreme expectations for yourself or others. Make sure you clearly express any expectations you may have with your family or work environment, whether it is in lengthy conversations or in writing. With this and the other suggestions from the previous chapters, you can experience a much happier and less difficult life.

## REVIEW

Expectations can either drive us forward to great accomplishments and relationships, or they can drag us down to discouragement and hopelessness. It is necessary to re-evaluate your own personal expectations and ensure they are realistically aligned towards the objectives you are trying to achieve. Likewise, it is crucial to terminate all assumed expectations we have towards others and their expectations of us.

He has a perfect plan for every one of us. Bring all your issues and questions to God. Thank Him for what He has done and what He is continually doing in your life. Place your expectations in Him and nothing more. Do not allow your past mistakes to get in the way of God's best. Do not let fear of failing keep you from pressing forward. God wants you to succeed and have a healthy and wealthy existence.

## PERSONAL APPLICATION

Take the time to evaluate what expectations you have placed on yourself and make sure they are realistic and achievable. Assess what expectations you have towards others in your life and make sure none of them are assumed. Equally discuss what expectations they have of you. You do not necessarily have to agree, but you will clear any presumptions they may have.

## SCRIPTURAL REFERENCES

Jeremiah 29:11

Philippians 4:6

1 John 5:15

Proverbs 3:6

Deuteronomy 31:6

Proverbs 22:6

## CHAPTER 8

# CONTROLLING OUR PERCEPTIONS

**THERE ARE A FEW** additional areas we should be conscious of as we continue our awareness of the destructive power of assumption. They are less common, but they occasionally occur.

## FIRST IMPRESSIONS

We have heard and understood the foundation principle of the importance of first impressions. When it involves appearing for an interview or when meeting other business people, we agree having a professional and clean look can be valuable. Unfortunately, many people assume who someone is based on their outward appearances or how they may carry themselves. It is important to present ourselves in a professional manner, but it does not make us who we are.

Research has shown that people are assessed within the first three seconds of an interaction with another. We all have first impressions of someone we meet. We have our own perspectives regarding what we think we see, and we are quick to judge. We form an opinion about someone without truly knowing anything about them. This immediate assumption can be wrong. When we label people, we use an immature form of thinking.

People are not always who we think we see in them. Our first intuition of others can be totally distorted by any number of things. That person's style, attitude, body language and comments may not have anything to do with that individual at all internally. It could, instead, have everything to do with what is going on in their own life at the time. I might walk into a restaurant and people may see "rocker" or "gothic," yet they do not realize I am a caring father of three children who believes in and loves God. They just see a man with long hair, jeans and a t-shirt. The same holds true if someone walks in a room and looks stylish, happy and approachable, but they could be the next serial killer at large.

We should not judge someone based on what they look like or how they present themselves. Jesus, in the book of John 7:20 in the Word, states not to judge based on appearances, but to judge correctly based on accurate and precise truth. If we resist our initial assumption towards others exterior, we have a chance to be aware of who a person truly is on the inside. Get all the facts before rushing into a conclusion. Communication and building a relationship with someone will help in understanding that person's actual value. Be careful not to allow first impressions to cause you to be guilty of assumption.

## JUDGING THE PAST

Our assumption of others can lead us into being judgmental. We may have heard or witnessed a mistake someone made in the past, and we quickly assumed they must be ill-behaved or they would never change. We condemn them before we know the truth about a matter or because they made a straightforward error. It is one thing to confront someone when we have observed them slipping up, as we see in the book of Matthew 18:15-18, but if we judge, criticize or hate people based on their history, we set ourselves up to be judged ourselves. We cannot be truly happy and content when we assume someone is horrible based on their past. We do not have to agree with them or like what they may have done, but we should not allow it to bring out the worst in ourselves.

I have viewed countless stories of how people

changed for the better. A woman's boyfriend used to be a drug dealer and an alcoholic. His past was nothing to be proud of, but he became a completely different person and cleaned up his life. His past mistakes are still there, but it does not mean he is that way now. He can only hope that people accept him and look at who he is today. If he learned from his mistakes and he is a better person, then his history should not matter.

One of my favorite scriptures in the bible is found in the book of Matthew 7:1-5. It describes how we can have a massive plank in our own eye, yet we try and remove a spec from another's. It is a classic description of how we can end up focusing on other peoples' mishaps without seeing our own issues we need to deal with. When we work on improving ourselves, we spend less time judging others, trying to repair or change them. There is plenty of work to do within ourselves. We need to shift our focus on being the best that we can be.

> When we work on improving ourselves, we spend less time judging others.

I understand it may be tough to forgive certain actions someone has committed. Maybe you feel like you cannot let go of how many times someone disappointed you. My only answer to this would be I want to continue being forgiven by God through the blood of Jesus, and I do not want to allow myself to enter into an unforgiving heart and risk having problems with God based on the book of Luke 6:36-38. Do you?

I encourage you to look for the best in others, which can bring out the best in yourself. You can set aside your own preconceived ideas about people and their intentions. Make sure you raise your consciousness as to what you think of others and ensure you do not enter into the dangers of assumption.

## PREVIOUS PERFORMANCES

Finally, do not set yourself up for disappointment by assuming someone will help you when you need it. Just because they are family or close friends, it is not good to place that type of expectation on them. There could be countless reasons why their help is not available, and just because they assisted you before, does not mean they will do it again. I have not only experienced frustration thinking I could count on someone to be there when I needed them most, but I have observed friends who were devastated when finding out their own family would not help them. The reasons are irrelevant, but we cannot place that sort of responsibility on someone in turn allowing ourselves to fall subject to disappointment.

Placing your trust in God is the best solution. Living by faith in God's Word and what He's promised is the only true resolution. Spend time meditating on the following scriptures from the bible: 1 Peter 5:7, Philippians 4:13-19, Matthew 6:33, Ephesians 3:20. You can be confident God is ready and able to hear your requests and help you beyond what you ask of Him. Seek Him first, and you can do everything through Christ, who is our ultimate strength.

## REVIEW

We should maintain our consciousness towards assumption in our fight to control it. Do not judge someone based on their appearances, but determine who that person is and what they are about correctly, based on accurate and precise truth through communication and relationship. Do not to allow first impressions to cause you to be responsible for assumption.

Do not place responsibilities on others by assuming someone will help you when you need it. You can pray to God to help you. Through His son, you can live by faith and get the strength and support you need to make it through anything.

## PERSONAL APPLICATION

Look for the best in others. It can bring out the best in you. Set aside your own preconceived ideas about people and their intentions, and you will be able to limit the negative results of entering into the dangers of assumption.

## SCRIPTURAL REFERENCES

John 7:20

Matthew 18:15-18

Matthew 7:1-5

Luke 6:36-38

1 Peter 5:7

Philippians 4:13-19

Matthew 6:33

Ephesians 3:20

## CHAPTER 9

# DO NOT OVERDO IT

**MY FAMILY** and I have become exceptionally sensitive to assumption and how to prevent it from causing problems. I thought it would be interesting to know how often it would show up in a standard day and share it with you. The results were intriguing.

## A DAY WITH ASSUMPTION

Unless I am traveling, I spend a lot of time in my home office. Whether I am producing television commercials and 3D intros or writing and researching on the web, I work on my computer. Being a single father of three kids, it helps to be home and available when they need me.

I spent a standard day focusing on everything which went on in our home to witness how many times assumption showed up. I am usually awake around four or five in the morning. As far back as the early nineties when I was in the military, I was up that early. It is amazing how much I can do before the rest of the world around me wakes up. I typically spend this time studying and working without interruptions.

This particular morning, I arose, moving about my usual routine, which involved turning my computer on and making a pot of coffee. I logged into my email account to check for messages, and a few minutes later returned to fill my cup with fresh coffee. I expected it to be done, but had forgotten to push the button. I smiled, shaking my head, and started the coffee maker.

*Looking for the best in others can bring out the best in you.*

My son's alarm went off at six o'clock. I figured he immediately got up and woke up his sisters. By six-thirty, I recognized it was still quiet, and the dog had not been taken outside. As I entered the hallway, I noticed the lights were still off. I woke the kids up and asked them to get ready for school. I did not want to leave any room assuming my son would remember to close the bathroom door before they left, so I re-confirmed it with him.

From the moment my children left until the time

the first group arrived at three-thirty, I stayed busy at the computer working on some projects. My girlfriend and I made plans for her to stop by and visit around five-thirty. I asked the kids to do their chores and my daughter to feed the dog. I wanted the house to look nice before my girlfriend's arrival. Fifteen minutes later, she called and said she was here.

Puzzled, I asked, "Didn't you say you would be here at five-thirty?"

"Yes," she answered, "But I thought I would come a little earlier."

I was happy she could make it earlier; but I had not finished my work, and the kids were in the middle of doing their chores. I shrugged it off and asked them to speed it up a bit.

My girlfriend and I were watching one of our favorite shows together. At the commercial break, I decided to check on the kids, make sure their homework was done and get a drink from the kitchen.

I quickly noticed the dog's bowls were empty and asked my daughter, "Why didn't you feed the dog?"

She said, "I thought you told Blaine to do it."

"No," I responded, "I asked you to do it. Please take care of it now."

As I was speaking to her, I saw her on a boys page on a network site.

I asked, "Who is that?"

She answered, "Oh, he's just some guy my friends told me about. They said he's kind of a jerk, but I was just checking out his page."

"How do you know he's a jerk?" I asked.

"I don't. That's just what they said." she responded.

Being conscious of assumption, I replied, "Well, you don't know him, and you can't go by what other people say. You know that."

I returned to the television area, and my girlfriend asked me where her drink was. I apologized. I did not know she wanted anything. I should have asked. I quickly returned with her drink, and we continued to watch the show.

After the program was over, she turned to me and said, "Baby. Why didn't you ask me if I wanted something to drink? You're usually good about stuff like that."

I quickly responded, "Why? Are you mad at me?"

Jokingly, she said, "Did I say that? Is that what you're assuming?"

We stared at each other for a brief moment in silence, and then we could no longer hold our laughter back.

As you can see, not including the time I spent working alone, there were around seven times within a total of about eight hours that some element of assumption entered into our day. It was an analysis of how assumption could show up in such a simple day. I thought I would share it with you.

### KEEP IT SIMPLE

My family has been aware of problems assumption can cause. We have worked hard and communicated through many issues to ensure we work on it daily. We manage it well now, but when we first began working on it, we saw it pop up all the time. Before you knew it, everyone was saying, "You're assuming, you're assuming!" We heard it in our house at least twenty times a day. We were so conscious of assumption, but it was getting out of hand. We had to understand how to handle it better and not howl "Assumption!" every time something was misinterpreted or misunderstood.

As the months went by, we noticed a lot less room for assumption to sneak in. We were aware of it, but we also knew how to attack and handle it better. Just because you know someone is assuming, does not mean you have to make it directly obvious. For example, when you are speaking with someone and you catch them, you do not have to say, "You're assuming too much." Just tell them you were misunderstood and clarify what you meant.

Another instance would be if you asked an employee to do something. Instead of saying, "I don't want to leave any room for assumptions, so could you repeat what I just said?" you can ask, "Do you mind repeating that to me please?" It is not necessary to overdo it, yet still handle your awareness and control of assumption. Just keep it simple as you continue to work in this area.

## CHAPTER 10

# ELIMINATING FEAR

**FEAR AND DOUBT** are the biggest enemies in our war against assumption. If we do not get rid of them, we will be too afraid to communicate or confront a situation. That will only result in our anger and frustration, ultimately complaining and speaking negative things into existence. We cannot allow fear and doubt to keep us from experiencing better things in life.

## WHAT IS FEAR?

Similar to assumption, fear is like a cancer. It starts small from thoughts caused by a situation or circumstance. It spreads like a virus, fully consuming our being. It begins to suffocate and paralyzes us, resulting in poor choices.

We can become depressed and miserable.

Fear is a painful emotion caused by an impending threat, evil, or pain. It is a doubt, concern or anxiety, which causes us to be afraid. When you operate in worry, you open the door to allow fear to manifest. If you become uncertain about a situation or what God has promised for you in His Word, you give fear permission to reside in your heart and cause problems in your decisions and life.

According to God's Word in the book of 2 Timothy 1:7, fear is a spirit. The spirit of fear does not come from God. God wishes for you to experience peace, not fear. In fact, it is impossible to please God in fear, and it keeps you from trusting Him because He wants you to have faith in Him and His Word (Hebrews 11:6). Faith is the opposite of fear (Mark 4:40). Fear also causes us to live in oppression. We become a slave to it according to Romans 8:15 and Hebrews 2:14-15.

> Do not underestimate the power that comes from the words you speak.

Living in fear can keep us from doing all that God has called us to do. It can keep us nailed to the floor, unable to move, hopeless and discouraged. If we do not deal with it, everything we fear can come to pass in our lives. Jesus paid the price for our freedom. You do not have to remain shackled in fear.

I suggest you do a further study on the subject

of fear and take the time to read the book of Job in the bible. One of the greatest examples I have seen in God's Word on the topic of fear comes from Job 3:25. He stated what he feared had come upon him. He had been so consumed by fear for years. Because of it, those things he was afraid of happened. He allowed fear to take hold of him and opened the door to destruction because Job chose to live in fear rather than faith in the promises of God. What I liked most was he never gave up on God and asked to be forgiven. He chose to get rid of fear. In the end, Job had everything he lost restored twice as much as he had before.

## THOUGHTS OF FEAR

Check your thought life. What scares you? What do you worry about? Are you afraid of not being good enough? Are you concerned about what people think about you? If not confronted, these anxieties can occupy your thought life, and those thoughts can change your character. They will lead to bad imaginations, which will result in acting on them.

When negative and fearful thoughts come into our mind, we need to deal with them right away. According to 2 Corinthians 10:5, you can eliminate those harmful thoughts and replace them with God's thoughts.

He does not desire you to be fearful, and He has promised to be your strength. Communicate your fears to God and leave them at His feet (1 Peter 5:7). He has promised to stand by you (Joshua 1:9, Isaiah 41:10). Do not allow negative thinking to torture you any longer. Renew your mind with good and positive thinking through the many great promises God has made to you. Get forceful over your thoughts of fear when they try to enter into your mind. You will have an easier time in confronting the areas of assumption.

## FEAR OF PEOPLE

One of the greatest fears I have witnessed is the fear of people. There are times in my life when I chose to do something contrary to what I believed because I feared how others would react. I failed to perform something God placed in my heart because I thought others would feel I was incompetent. As a result of allowing myself to be influenced by others' opinions, I made many mistakes that caused hardships. I became unproductive for God. It took me a long time to realize you cannot please everyone. Some-body will disapprove of you no matter what you achieve. I knew it was time to be free from my bondage to people and shift my efforts to pleasing God (Psalms 118:6).

The story in the bible that is a great example of

being in bondage to people is found in the chapter of 1 Samuel 15. Through the prophet Samuel, King Saul was given precise instructions to destroy every living thing in a city. Unfortunately, he did not complete the task as ordered. When confronted by God, King Saul confessed his fear of the people he ruled (1 Samuel 15:24). Instead of pleasing God, he tried to satisfy the people, which resulted in losing his kingdom.

If you try to please people, you will not be able to please God. If you have had problems in this area, do not allow yourself to struggle with it any more (Galatians 1:10). Stop striving to please others and start living by faith and pleasing God (Hebrews 11:6). Doing so can help make controlling assumption effortless.

## THINK AND SPEAK POSITIVELY

Do not underestimate the power that comes from the words you speak. Whatever you meditate on and say out loud is what can happen. Negative things will occur and bad thoughts will come. It is unavoidable, but you do not have to allow them to inhabit your mind. You do not need to keep those thoughts. You can eliminate them by not speaking them out. It is more beneficial to say something good and positive, instead of keeping silent and meditating on those bad thoughts. Interrupt your negative thinking by verbalizing good things, especially God's promises. In order to do this, we need to meditate on God's Word so we can replace the negative thoughts with positive ones. It will allow us to renew our minds to turn fear into faith and please God instead of people (Hebrews 11:6, Romans 10:17).

If you make a mistake, do not beat yourself up over it. Just change your thinking about it and move on. Do not let worry and condemnation destroy what you are working on. Get back up and try it again. Make a decision to abolish fear, have confidence in God's promises, live the best you can and speak good things.

## REVIEW

Fear and doubt are the biggest enemies in our fight against assumption. If we do not put an end them, we will be too afraid to communicate or confront a situation. Similar to assumption, fear is like a cancer. It starts small from thoughts caused by a situation or circumstance. It spreads like a virus fully consuming our being.

Fear is a painful emotion caused by an impending threat, evil, and pain. It is a doubt, concern or anxiety, which causes us to be afraid. Living in fear can keep us from all that God has called us to do. It can keep us nailed to the floor, unable to move, fully hopeless and discouraged. You do not have to remain shackled in fear. Jesus paid the price for our freedom.

If you try to please people, you will not be able to please God. If you have had problems in this area, do not allow yourself to struggle with it any more. Stop striving to please others, and start living by faith and pleasing God.

You can get rid of harmful thoughts and replace them with God's thoughts. Do not underestimate the power that comes from the words you speak. Whatever you meditate on and say out loud is what can happen. Instead, say something good and positive, as an alternative to keeping silent and meditating on those bad thoughts.

Interrupt your negative thinking by verbalizing positive words, especially God's promises.

## PERSONAL APPLICATION

Check your thought life. Make a quality decision not to let any anxieties occupy your mind and not to act on them. Study God's Word and renew your mind with good and positive thinking.

## SCRIPTURAL REFERENCES

2 Timothy 1:7

Hebrews 11:6

Mark 4:40

Romans 8:15

Hebrews 2:14-15

Job 3:25

2 Corinthians 10:5

1 Peter 5:7

Joshua 1:9

Isaiah 41:10

Psalms 118:6

1 Samuel 15

Galatians 1:10

Romans 10:17

C H A P T E R   1 1

# CONCLUSION

**THE FOCUS** of this book was to show you how to understand the destructive power of assumption and how to control it in every part of your life. It is essential that we know how to do this, because we all have areas we can improve on when it comes to how we hear, receive or comprehend certain things.

No matter how much you clean your house, it does not guarantee roaches won't come in. Fortunately, there are other things you can do to get rid of them when they show up. Assumption is the same way. Do not ignore the fact that it will show up on occasion. Be prepared to confront it and communicate at all times.

## LET GO OF PAST MISTAKES

Life is tough enough; each day brings its own issues along with it. We don not have to make it worse by allowing assumption to flood our lives. Forget your past mistakes. Let them go. Ask God to forgive you and move forward from here.

Don't ever let anyone tear you down and make you feel like you are worthless. It does not matter what they think. God thinks only great things of you and has a perfect path for your life. You do not have to please anyone but Him. Whether it is your family, friends or co-workers, it is not worth allowing what they feel about you to live in constant worry and fear. Do not surround yourself with people who do not support you or who make you feel inadequate when you are around them. Associate yourself with good, loving people who are supportive and kind.

## ACCEPT YOURSELF

Accept yourself for who you are. It is okay to be different. In fact, it is very rewarding not to be like everyone else. Do what feels right to you within the limits of God's Word. For example, if you feel overweight, workout for yourself and to be healthy, not because your family, friends, or the media says you should. Thank God for what He has created in you and love yourself.

Read Proverbs 3:5, Philippians 4:6-8, and Colossians 3:12. Enjoy life to its fullest and follow your dreams. Pursue what you believe God has called you to accomplish. May God bless and enrich you in all you do.

## CHAPTER 12

# STEPS TO SALVATION

**IN CASE** you are not saved, I want to make available to you the steps you can take to be born into the Kingdom of God and be saved. If you wish to re-dedicate your life again to God, because you have wandered away from Him, for whatever reason, you can go to the end of this chapter and speak the simple prayer. God is real, and He loves you beyond your imagination. You can take this opportunity to begin fresh.

## 1. RECOGNIZE AND ADMIT YOU ARE A SINNER

You must first recognize and admit you are a sinner. Everyone born into this world is a sinner. It is not necessarily because you have done something wrong, but because of Adam's decision in the Garden of Eden, when his sin separated him from God. Being descendants of Adam, we are born sinners and must be born again. Reference: Romans 5: 12-14 and Psalm 51:5. You must recognize you are a sinner, admit to it and be saved.

## 2. REPENT OF YOUR SINS

Change your mind and the direction of your heart by repenting of all your sins and make a one hundred and eighty degree turn - away from sin, to a life agreeable to God. It does not mean you are just sorry, but you make a quality decision to ask God for His forgiveness and to cleanse you of all unrighteousness according to 1 John 1:9.

## 3. CONFESS JESUS AS LORD AND SAVIOR

Confess Jesus Christ as your supreme authority over your life. Believe that He lived on this earth, was crucified and buried and raised from the dead by God for the forgiveness of your sins. Speak out loud that He is your Lord and Savior according to the book of Romans 10:9.

## 4. BE BAPTIZED

Matthew 3:6 says you must be baptized in water. It is a representation of the death, burial and resurrection of Jesus Christ, who was also baptized in water. You wipe out all of your old lifestyle of sin and death and become as white as snow, dying too yourself and becoming a new creation in Christ Jesus, now with the Holy Spirit living in you. All old things are passed away and all things become new. Reference: Romans 6:3-11 and 2 Corinthians 5:17.

According to John 14:15-26, the Holy Spirit now lives in you, and you have Him as your Comforter, Teacher and Guide. You can also receive the Baptism of the Holy Spirit based on Luke 24:49 and Acts 1:4-8, which gives you His ability and adds it to your abilities. The evidence of this lies in your speaking in an unknown, spiritual tongue, according to Acts 2:1-4 in order to amplify your English tongue to a perfected prayer, praying from your spirit to God's Spirit. Reference Romans 8:26, Jude 1:20-21 and 1 Corinthians 14:2.

### Receiving the Baptism of the Holy Spirit Steps:

1. (Acts 2:1-4) Understand the Holy Spirit is a gift which was given on the day of Pentecost.
2. (Acts 2:38) Realize salvation is the only requirement necessary for receiving the Holy Spirit.
3. (Acts 8:17; 19:6) Know the laying on of hands is scriptural.
4. (1 Corinthians 14:13-14) Expect to speak in tongues when hands are laid on you.

5. (Luke 11:11-13) Disregard all fears or false teaching about receiving a counterfeit.

6. (Romans 8:26; Ephesians 6:18) Open your mouth as an act of faith.

7. (1 Corinthians 14:33) Receive the gift of speaking in tongues in an atmosphere of serenity.

## 5. OBEY GOD'S WORD

Spend time reading the Bible and meditate on God's Word, so you understand how to live according to His ways. Therefore, you make His Word the foundation and final authority in your life. Reference: Proverbs 3:1-4 and 1 John 5:3.

## SPEAK THIS PRAYER TO BE SAVED

Say this prayer out loud: *"Heavenly father in heaven. I recognize that I was born a sinner and I admit it. I confess to you with my mouth that I turn away from my sins, and I believe in my heart that Jesus Christ is Lord. I believe that He lived on this earth, was crucified for my sins and was raised from the dead for my salvation. I accept and receive my salvation now. Thank you for coming into my life today. I believe I am now the righteousness of God. Through the blood and in the name of Jesus Christ I pray. Amen."*

Congratulations and welcome to the Christian family. You just accepted Jesus Christ into your life!

## SPEAK THIS PRAYER TO RE-DEDICATE

Say this prayer out loud: *"Heavenly Father in heaven. I have committed sins against you and the Holy Spirit. I have performed sins of commission and omission. I repent for all my sins and ask you to forgive me through the blood of Jesus. As you forgive me, I forgive all those who have sinned against me. I make a decision to follow your Word and live according to it. I re-dedicate my life to you. Thank you in name of Jesus Christ I pray. Amen."*

## ABOUT THE AUTHOR

Gregory Dollar is an author, contemporary speaker and musician who has been directing and producing in Christian Television for well over a decade. In 2008, he stepped into his calling to minister the gospel to a new generation of teens and suffering adults. He is a supporter of Do Something and Youth Noise. He has one son and two daughters.

Gregory can be found at "gregorydollar" on Twitter or "gregdollar" on Facebook. You can also visit his web site at www.gregorydollar.com.

## MEDIA RESOURCES AND CONTACT

For a Complete List of Resources
or to Schedule the Author for
Speaking Engagements, Contact

Gregory Dollar
greg@gregdollar.com
www.gregorydollar.com

NOTES

LaVergne, TN USA
08 March 2011
219305LV00001B/11/P